This book is dedicated:

To my mom, who developed my work ethic.

To my husband, Charlie, who breathes confidence into everything I do.

To my children, Nicholas and Christina, who
fill my life with the joys of family.

And to my dear furry friend Clydie, who loved me unconditionally.

Contents

Foreword viii

Preface x

Introduction xi

Chapter 1 Parents: Social Factors for Learning Mathematics 1

Teacher Inquiry for Knowing and Supporting Parents with Mathematics 2

Teacher Inquiry Approaches 3

Planning Your Inquiry Journey 4

Supporting Parents through the Grades 5

References 13

Chapter 2 Surfacing Perspectives through Surveying 15

Survey 1: Purpose 16

Survey 1 16

Survey 1: Findings 18

Survey 1: Responsive Action Steps 20

Survey 2: Purpose 20

Survey 2 21

Survey 2: Findings 22

Survey 2: Responsive Action Steps 23

Survey 3: Purpose 24

Survey 3 25

Survey 3: Findings 27

	Survey 3: Responsive Action Steps	28
	Planning Your Survey Inquiry	29
	Supporting Parents through the Grades	31
	References	36
Chapter 3	Witnessing Parent-Child Interactions through Observation	37
	Determining What to Observe	38
	Gathering Families	38
	Engaging Families	42
	Taking Field Notes	42
	Planning Your Observation Inquiry	45
	Supporting Parents through the Grades	46
	References	47
Chapter 4	Digging Deeper through Interviewing	49
	Conducting Interviews	51
	Findings and Responsive Action Steps	53
	Planning Your Interview Inquiry	58
	Supporting Parents through the Grades	59
	References	60
Chapter 5	Anchor Tasks for Families	61
	Anchor Task 1: Concept Cards	61
	Anchor Task 2: Attribute Pieces	64
	Anchor Task 3: Pattern Blocks	65
	Anchor Task 4: Perimeter and Area	66
	Anchor Task 5: Finding Pi	67
	Anchor Task 6: Monster Combos	68
	Anchor Task 7: Let's Talk Pizza!	70

Chapter 6 Learning as a Teacher Inquiry Group about Parents
           and Mathematics   73

           Collective Learning Framework 1   74

           Collective Learning Framework 2   77

           References   80

Foreword

At the start of the 2013 school year, Linda Gojak, president of the National Council of Teachers of Mathematics, exhorted teachers to partner with parents. She wrote: "The need for our students to be successful in mathematics is more urgent than at any time in recent history. In this era of focus on college, career, and life readiness, engaging parents is critical to the success of students from pre-kindergarten through high school." Gojak recommends that "just as we plan daily instruction for our students, a specific yearlong plan to get parents involved and supportive of their children will positively influence our work and can only lead to increased student success."

Effective teacher-parent-student partnerships are consistently cited as hallmarks of effective schools—helping students do better in school, stay in school longer, and like school more. But even for teachers named Jack or Jacqueline, effective partnerships do not magically spring forth from the ground. They need to be carefully seeded, tended, and cared for.

In her book *Using Teacher Inquiry for Knowing and Supporting Parents with Mathematics*, Dr. Regina Mistretta provides teachers with seeds (e.g., anchor workshop activities) and a collection of gardening tools to grow and nourish a garden of interactions between a child and his/her parent (e.g., ready to duplicate and use survey forms, invitations to parent-child sessions, observation forms, useful websites, as well as specific suggestions about using materials in her book). Teachers' gardens will yield fruits such as richer, more helpful parent-child math talk, which in turn will enhance children's understandings and skills, improve their performance, and build confidence and pride in doing maths.

Using Teacher Inquiry for Knowing and Supporting Parents with Mathematics

Regina M. Mistretta

ROWMAN & LITTLEFIELD
Lanham • Boulder • New York • London

Published by Rowman & Littlefield
A wholly owned subsidiary of The Rowman & Littlefield Publishing Group, Inc.
4501 Forbes Boulevard, Suite 200, Lanham, Maryland 20706
www.rowman.com

16 Carlisle Street, London W1D 3BT, United Kingdom

British Library Cataloguing in Publication Information Available   .

Library of Congress Cataloging-in-Publication Data Available

ISBN 978-1-4758-1257-2 (hardcover)
ISBN 978-1-4758-1258-9 (paperback)
ISBN 978-1-4758-1259-6 (e-book)

∞™ The paper used in this publication meets the minimum requirements of American National Standard for Information Sciences—Permanence of Paper for Printed Library Materials, ANSI/NISO Z39.48-1992.

Printed in the United States of America

Dr. Mistretta's book is the culmination of over a dozen years of her scholarly work on teacher-parent-student collaborations. Her work builds on relevant current research and, most important, on her firsthand action research with teachers and their students and parents in a variety of public and parochial school settings. The inquiry approaches and findings she shares in her book serve as a means for improving both parent-student and parent-teacher communication about mathematics teaching and learning.

I am particularly pleased that Dr. Mistretta asked me to prepare this foreword. She and I have had special connections ever since she was a middle school math teacher at St. Anselm and a student in my graduate math education research courses at Brooklyn College, where I taught for over thirty-five years. After obtaining her doctorate at Columbia University, also my doctoral alma mater, she taught as an adjunct faculty colleague with me at Brooklyn College, before beginning her career in mathematics education at St. John's University.

For some of her anchor activities, Dr. Mistretta chose highly motivational and proven math tasks (e.g., Attribute Pieces, Today's Date, Which One Doesn't Belong) from *Teaching Mathematics in Elementary School*, a widely used mathematics methods book (1979) I coauthored with Rosamond Welchman-Tischler. Dr. Mistretta has told me often about her successful uses of that book in her math education courses at St. John's University and in professional-development math workshops.

Teachers take pride in the successes of their students. I have enjoyed following Dr. Mistretta's professional maturation over the years, from sixth-grade math teacher to professor in education at St John's University. Based on her outstanding record of research and publications, she is recognized among mathematics educators as an expert on teacher-parent-student collaborations. As a result of her collaborations with classroom teachers in the New York City area, she has built a reputation as a helpful resource in school mathematics.

My congratulations to her on authoring a book that provides guidance to teachers and others interested in parent-child interactions in mathematics. Her book guides readers to grow their own "in the know" expertise about parent-child interactions, and to find ways to harvest their knowledge and use it throughout the school year to positively influence their students' performance in mathematics. Also, I believe that many "in the know" teachers will be inspired to build on their success with math parent-child collaborations and plant and harvest crops in other subject areas as well.

Dr. David Fuys,
Professor of Mathematics Education (retired), Brooklyn College

~

Preface

As a parent, waiting for my children on the school corner at dismissal time, I often heard parents' pleas for help concerning their child's learning of mathematics. Parents were frustrated over how mathematics was being taught; they learned differently, and felt helpless when trying to assist their child with homework.

There were parents who questioned whether or not teachers even knew what they were doing. I learned how some parents assisted their child in unproductive ways. Others supported their child in very meaningful ways. I continued to listen to how parents were assisting their child, the challenges parents faced, and how they wanted teachers' support—all the time saying to myself: If only the teachers could come to know about what I am hearing. It is for this reason that I wrote this book—for you, the teachers.

The more teachers *know* about parents and mathematics, the better they can *support* parents. I wrote this book to serve as a teacher's inquiry guide for investigating parent-child interactions with mathematics, and how best to support those interactions. Inquiry approaches and related tools used by teachers, myself included, to attain a state of being that I term "in the know" about parents and mathematics are shared.

I invite you to embark on an inquiry journey with this book, either individually or collectively with your colleagues. Engage in surveying, observing, and/or interviewing classroom families, and read about what other teachers have found out and acted upon. The goal for everyone reading and using this book is to build strong bridges between home and school, and ultimately support children's learning of mathematics.

~

Introduction

This book is organized to serve as a teacher's inquiry guide for deeply knowing about *how* and *why* classroom parents assist their child in mathematics the way they do. Such knowledge informs how teachers support parents as positive social factors who can influence their child's mathematics achievement.

In chapter 1 the importance of teachers viewing parents as academic resources for children's learning of mathematics is explained. Teacher inquiry is underscored as a critical step toward meaningfully supporting parents in such a role. A mindset, referred to as "in the know" about parents and mathematics, is described, and teacher inquiry approaches for developing that mindset are introduced. Questions are posed for consideration while planning to inquire about parents and mathematics, and resources for supporting parents through the grades are shared.

In chapter 2 descriptions of how surveying can serve as a means for investigating parents' perspectives on their child's mathematics education are provided. Three field-tested surveys are included and coupled with teachers' findings and responsive action steps. Questions are posed and suggestions offered for consideration while planning to survey, and resources for supporting parents through the grades with mathematics are shared.

In chapter 3 observation is described as a means for witnessing how parents and children work together on mathematical tasks. Forms of parent-child interaction to note while observing are explained and coupled with teachers' findings and responsive action steps. Questions are posed and suggestions are offered for consideration while planning to observe, and chapter-related resources for supporting parents through the grades with mathematics are shared.

In chapter 4 interviewing is explained as a means for deepening one's inquiry findings about parents and mathematics. Questions to ask during interviews are included and coupled with teachers' findings and responsive action steps. Questions are posed and suggestions offered for consideration while planning to interview, and resources for supporting parents through the grades with mathematics are shared.

Chapter 5 includes anchor tasks for connecting parents with school mathematics throughout the grades. The tasks support parents' familiarity with mathematics content, and provide entry points for parents to engage in conversation with their child about mathematical thinking. In chapter 6 teachers' collective inquiry concerning parents and mathematics is explained. Two professional learning frameworks are described.

One framework focuses on using survey, observation, and/or interview findings about parents and mathematics. The other framework involves using best-practice publications about parents and mathematics. Guidelines for structuring related Teacher Inquiry Groups are provided, and questions for guiding the group's collective learning are offered.

My intention is to illuminate for readers the power of inquiry as a tool for knowing and supporting parents with mathematics. Prior to using the inquiry approaches shared in this book, teachers need to explain the purpose for an inquiry approach to parents and obtain parents' permission to use an inquiry approach as a means of supporting them with mathematics.

CHAPTER ONE

~

Parents: Social Factors for Learning Mathematics

In this chapter the importance of teachers viewing parents as academic resources for children's learning of mathematics is explained. Teacher inquiry is underscored as a critical step toward meaningfully supporting parents in such a role. A mindset, referred to as "in the know" about parents and mathematics, is described, and teacher inquiry approaches for developing that mindset are introduced. In conclusion, questions are posed for you to ponder while planning to inquire about parents and mathematics at your school setting. Chapter-related resources for supporting parents through the grades are shared as well.

We don't know how to help our children anymore. The way I was taught to approach certain problems is not how kids are taught to approach them today. The way kids are taught today is more conceptual and inquiry-based, whereas we [parents] learned in a more direct way, sort of "here's how you solve this problem, now do it."

Eighth-Grade Parent, Bronx, New York

Parents, meaning all adults who play an active role in a child's home life, are those social factors that can support children's learning of mathematics. For example, when parents assist their child by posing thought-provoking questions or breaking down a problem into smaller, more manageable pieces, they help organize their child's mathematical thinking (Walker, Shenker, and Hoover-Dempsey 2010).

When parents adjust their assistance to match their child's current abilities, they help scaffold their child's thinking to higher levels. In addition, when parents create home-learning environments that nurture self-confidence, they help reduce their child's mathematics anxiety, and, in turn, position them for academic success, especially with higher-order domains of mathematics (Vukovic, Roberts, and Wright 2013).

It is these parental forms of assistance that depict the "quality" of assistance parents give to their child that is just as important, if not more, as the quantity of that assistance. This quality, though, hinges on teachers' support of parents. Parents can face challenges concerning their child's mathematical learning. For example, this chapter's representative opening quote from an eighth-grade parent illuminates how unfamiliarity with current ways of teaching mathematics can limit parents' engagement in their child's learning.

This unfamiliarity, at times, can lead to parents unraveling at home what is learned in the classroom. For example, when parents are unfamiliar with current content and methodology, they tend to resist reform efforts (Remillard and Jackson 2006). Rather than reinforce their child's learning environment, they assist in ways that only mirror their own past learning environment.

Teachers need to support parents' familiarity with current mathematics standards and ways of teaching it; they need to share productive strategies with parents for assisting their child's learning of mathematics at home. However, it is essential for teachers to provide such support in ways that both respond to parents' needs as well as acknowledge and respect parents' knowledge and experiences (Civil and Andrade 2003). Therefore, I promote inquiry as a means for deeply knowing classroom parents' perspectives and skill sets concerning mathematics education, and supporting them in meaningful and inclusive ways.

Teacher Inquiry for Knowing and Supporting Parents with Mathematics

Teachers are what I call "in the know" about parents and mathematics when they understand *how* and *why* parents and children work together the way they do on mathematical tasks such as daily homework and projects. Such a mindset positions teachers to respond to the essential "subtle aspects of parental involvement" (Jeynes 2010).

These aspects include parental expectations for their children's success with mathematics, the quality of parent-child communication, and parents' style when assisting their children's mathematical learning. Responsiveness to these aspects of parental involvement is critical since children's achievement in school depends on multiple contexts, including activities and interactions between parents and their children at home and in their communities in an active and multidirectional manner (Epstein 1987).

Parent-child interactions can differ socially, culturally, and linguistically, warranting teacher inquiry as a means for determining how best to support parents' diverse needs (Civil 2012). Otherwise, parent support structures may only mirror a one-size-fits-all approach that can actually place support for *all* parents at risk.

Inquiry also minimizes misinterpretations of parents' actions or lack of them. For example, parents' low level of involvement is sometimes misunderstood as lack of commitment when it is actually a lack of understanding content and/or ways of teaching that content. Such misinterpretations lend themselves to positioning parents as outsiders looking in, rather than as active participants who meaningfully contribute to their child's academic learning. In turn, parental feelings of disempowerment can develop barriers between home and school, often resulting in parents reinforcing rote procedures with their child without deepening understanding of the procedures' derivation and application.

Teacher Inquiry Approaches

The teacher inquiry approaches described in this book serve to inform the ways you as teacher develop supportive relationships. These approaches—namely, surveying, observing, and interviewing—are explained in chapters 2, 3, and 4. Each of these chapters includes related findings and responsive action steps of mine as well as those teacher inquirers with whom I have collaborated.

These inquiry approaches are not meant to exist in isolation from one another; rather, I encourage you to use all of them on your journey toward acquiring deep understandings of parent-child interactions with mathematics. For example, specific parent perspectives you discover through a survey can be clarified and/or expanded upon through observations and interviews.

Your collection of data should also not be thought of as existing independently from your data analysis. Your data collection should also not be conducted in a linear, lockstep manner. As stated by Nancy Fichtman Dana (2013), data collection and data analysis are iterative in nature. As you collect your data, you should seek to understand what your data is telling you about parents and mathematics. In turn, you should make informed decisions about how to support parents and what next steps to take on your inquiry journey about parents and mathematics.

It is understood that diverse circumstances exist; therefore, the intent of this book is to offer methods of inquiry for your direct use or adaptation as you journey toward being "in the know" about parents and mathematics. The approaches you use to inquire will vary according to your individual professional settings and personal preferences. Diverse situations will also determine whether you inquire individually or collectively, as explained in chapter 5. The common, unifying factor, though, is that all who take this journey arrive positioned to support parents as children's academic partners at home who, in turn, reinforce the learning environment cultivated at school.

Following are representative comments from teachers who took the journey.

- "My overall findings have influenced my teaching. Reaching out to parents has opened a line of communication that has informed how I approach my students as individuals."
- "I'm deeply aware now of the difficulties parents face, and consistently reflect on ways to better incorporate parents into the mathematics learning process."
- "I learned with and from parents. I came to know about so many 'back stories' that have informed my understandings of students' behaviors and parents' talents."
- "Although my high school parents want their children to succeed in their mathematical learning, they are not likely to knock down my classroom door to talk with me directly about their child's mathematics education. However, I did learn through my interviews with parents about their receptiveness to requests I make. For example, if I convey to my parents the rationale for their child explaining answers, my parents *will* encourage this practice at home. I found out that parents do care, and are receptive to my support."

Planning Your Inquiry Journey

Main points are summarized in this section of each chapter, and questions are posed for you to ponder as a means of both reviewing chapter content and guiding your inquiry about parents and mathematics.

- Parents are those social factors that can support children's learning of mathematics. The "quality" of assistance is just as important, if not more, as the quantity of assistance.

- ◆ How do you define "quality" parental assistance in mathematics?
- ◆ What aspects of your definition do you wonder about?
- Parents' low level of involvement can sometimes be misunderstood as lack of commitment, as opposed to an actual lack of familiarity with content and/or ways of teaching that content.
  - ◆ Which parental behaviors might you inquire about to avoid such misinterpretation?

Supporting Parents through the Grades

I, as well as teachers with whom I have worked over the past twelve years, have crafted and/or selected resources to support parents' familiarity with mathematics teaching and learning at different levels in their child's academic career. These resources that are shared below can also be found online at www.http://tinyurl.com/ltpw6af in both Word document and PowerPoint presentation formats.

You can use the information in crafting informational packets, individual pieces of correspondence, and/or PowerPoint slides for presentation purposes. In addition, all resources reflect the content and pedagogical practices advocated in the Common Core State Standards for Mathematics (CCSSM 2010).

Textbox 1.1. Shifts in Classroom Environment

Away From	Toward
Classrooms as collections of individuals	Classrooms as mathematics communities
Teacher as "sole authority" for right answers	*Logic and mathematical evidence as verification*
Mere memorization of procedures	Mathematical reasoning
Emphasis on mechanistic finding of answers	*Conjecturing, inventing, and problem solving*
Treating mathematics as a body of isolated concepts and procedures	Connecting mathematics, its ideas, and applications

K	1	2	3	4	5	6	7	8	HS
Counting & Cardinality									
Number and Operations in Base Ten						Ratios and Proportional Relationships			Number & Quantity
			Number and Operations – Fractions			The Number System			
Operations and Algebraic Thinking						Expressions and Equations			Algebra
								Functions	Functions
Geometry									Geometry
Measurement and Data						Statistics and Probability			Statistics & Probability

Figure 1.1. Common Core State Standards Mathematics Domain Progression (CCSSM 2010)

Table 1.1. Priorities in Support of Rich Instruction and Expectations of Fluency and Conceptual Understanding (CCSSM 2010)

Grade	Priority
K–2	Addition and subtraction; measurement using whole number quantities
3–5	Multiplication and division of whole numbers and fractions
6	Ratios and proportional reasoning; early expressions and equations
7	Ratios and proportional reasoning; arithmetic of rational numbers
8	Linear algebra

Table 1.2. Key Fluencies (CCSSM 2010)

Grade	Required Fluency
K	Add/subtract within 5
1	Add/subtract within 10 Add/subtract within 20
2	Add/subtract within 100 (paper and pencil)
3	Multiply/divide within 100 Add/subtract within 1,000
4	Add/subtract within 1,000,000
5	Multi-digit multiplication Multi-digit division
6	Multi-digit decimal operation
7	Solve $px + q = r$, $p(x + q) = r$
8	Solve simple 2×2 systems by inspection

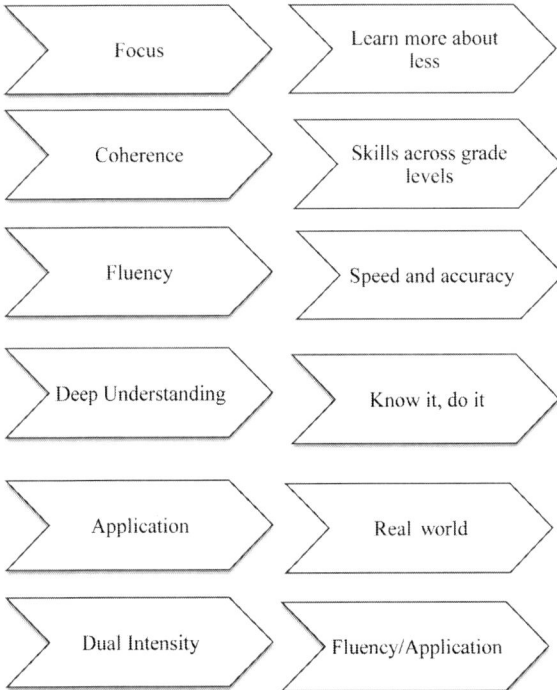

Focus	Learn more about less
Coherence	Skills across grade levels
Fluency	Speed and accuracy
Deep Understanding	Know it, do it
Application	Real world
Dual Intensity	Fluency/Application

Figure 1.2. Common Core Shifts in Mathematics (CCSSM 2010)

Table 1.3. Mathematics Shift 1: Focus (Learn more about less) (EngageNY.org)

What the Student Does . . .	What the Teacher Does . . .	Parents Can . . .
• Spends more time on fewer concepts	• Focuses instructional time on priority concepts	• Know what the priority work is for your child for their grade level • Spend time with your child on priority work • Ask your child's teacher about their progress on priority work

Table 1.4. Mathematics Shift 2: Coherence (Skills across grade levels) (EngageNY.org)

What the Student Does . . .	What the Teacher Does . . .	Parents Can . . .
• Builds on knowledge from year to year, in a coherent learning progression	• Connects the math focus areas across grade levels • Connects to the way content was taught the year before and the years after • Focuses on priority progressions	• Be aware of what your child struggled with last year and how that will affect learning this year

Table 1.5. Mathematics Shift 3: Fluency (Speed and accuracy) (EngageNY.org)

What the Student Does . . .	What the Teacher Does . . .	Parents Can . . .
• Spends time practicing skills, with intensity (in high volume)	• Supports students to know basic skills at a greater level of fluency • Focuses on the listed fluencies by grade level • Uses high-quality problem sets, in high volume	• Support children to know/ memorize basic math facts • Know all of the fluencies for your child's grade level, and prioritize learning of those fluencies in need of mastery

Table 1.6. Mathematics Shift 4: Deep Understanding (Know it, do it) (EngageNY.org)

What the Student Does . . .	What the Teacher Does . . .	Parents Can . . .
• Shows mastery of material at a deep level of understanding • Articulates mathematical reasoning both verbally and in written form • Demonstrates deep conceptual understanding of priority concepts • Demonstrates understanding of why the mathematics works through modeling, verbal explanation, and/or written justification	• Creates opportunities for students to understand mathematical concepts and procedures from a variety of entry points • Ensures that every student understands the material before moving on to further topics	• Notice whether your child really knows why the answer is what it is through conversation and written work • Provide opportunities for your child to discuss mathematics at home • Know the mathematics your child needs to know

Table 1.7. Mathematics Shift 5: Application (Real world) (EngageNY.org)

What the Student Does . . .	What the Teacher Does . . .	Parents Can . . .
• Applies mathematics in other content areas and situations, as relevant • Chooses the right mathematical concept and/or procedure to solve a problem when not necessarily prompted to do so • Applies math in real-world situations • Knows which mathematical concepts and/or procedures to use for varied situations	• Applies mathematics to other academic disciplines • Provides students with real-world experiences and opportunities to apply what they have learned	• Point out everyday applications of mathematics • Ask your child to do the mathematics involved that come up in their daily life

Table 1.8. Mathematics Shift 6: Dual Intensity (Fluency/Application) (EngageNY.org)

What the Student Does . . .	What the Teacher Does . . .	Parents Can . . .
• Practices mathematics basic facts and skills with an intensity that results in fluency • Applies mathematics conceptual understandings and procedural skills in novel situations	• Provides balanced instruction concerning mathematical concepts, procedural skills, and problem solving • Expects students to demonstrate conceptual understandings, procedural skills (including mastery of basic facts), and problem-solving abilities involving real-life applications	• Notice areas your child has strengths and weaknesses; address the weak areas with your child's teacher • Make sure your child is practicing basic mathematics facts he/she struggles with • Make sure your child is thinking about mathematics in real life; he/she should be speaking and writing about their mathematical thinking

---

Textbox 1.2.
K–12 Standards for Mathematical Practice (CCSSM 2010)

1. Make sense of problems and persevere in solving them.
2. Reason abstractly and quantitatively.
3. Construct viable arguments and critique the reasoning of others.
4. Model with mathematics.
5. Use appropriate tools strategically.
6. Attend to precision.
7. Look for and make use of structure.
8. Look for and express regularity in repeated reasoning.

Table 1.9. Mathematical Practice 1 (CCSSM 2010)

Description	Expected Student Behaviors
Make sense of problems and persevere in solving them	• Explain the meaning of a problem • Describe possible approaches to a solution • Consider similar problems to gain insights • Use concrete objects or illustrations to think about and solve problems • Monitor and evaluate their progress and change strategy if needed • Check their answers using a different method

Table 1.10. Mathematical Practice 2 (CCSSM 2010)

Description	Expected Student Behaviors
Reason abstractly and quantitatively	• Explain the relationship between quantities in problem situations • Represent situations using symbols (e.g., writing expressions or equations) • Create representations that fit the problem • Use flexibly the different properties of equations and objects

Table 1.11. Mathematical Practice 3 (CCSSM 2010)

Description	Expected Student Behaviors
Construct viable arguments and critique the reasoning of others	• Understand and use assumptions, definitions, and previous results to explain and justify solutions • Make conjectures by building a logical set of statements • Analyze situations and use counter-examples • Justify conclusions in a way that is understandable to teachers and peers • Compare two possible arguments for strengths and weaknesses

Table 1.12. Mathematical Practice 4 (CCSSM 2010)

Description	Expected Student Behaviors
Model with mathematics	• Apply mathematics to solve problems in real life • Make assumptions and approximations to simplify a problem • Identify important quantities and use tools to map their relationships • Reflect on the reasonableness of their answer based on the context of the problem

Table 1.13. Mathematical Practice 5 (CCSSM 2010)

Description	Expected Student Behaviors
Use appropriate tools strategically	• Consider a variety of tools and choose the appropriate tool (e.g., manipulative, ruler, technology) to support their problem solving • Use estimation to detect possible errors • Use technology to help visualize, explore, and compare information

Table 1.14. Mathematical Practice 6 (CCSSM 2010)

Description	Expected Student Behaviors
Attend to precision	• Communicate precisely using clear definitions and appropriate mathematics language • State the meanings of symbols • Specify appropriate units of measure and labels of axes • Use a degree of precision appropriate for the problem context

Table 1.15. Mathematical Practice 7 (CCSSM 2010)

Description	Expected Student Behaviors
Look for and make use of structure	• Explain mathematical patterns or structures • Shift perspective and see things as single objects or as composed of several objects • Explain why and when properties of operations are true in context

Table 1.16. Mathematical Practice 8 (CCSSM 2010)

Description	Expected Student Behaviors
Look for and express regularity in repeated reasoning	• Notice if calculations are repeated and use information to solve problems • Use and justify the use of general methods or shortcuts • Self-assess to see whether a strategy makes sense as they work, checking for reasonableness prior to getting the answer

References

Civil, Marta. "Mathematics Teaching and Learning of Immigrant Students: An Overview of the Research Field across Multiple Settings." In *Critique and Politics of Mathematics Education*, edited by B. Greer and O. Skovsmose, 127–42. New York: Routledge, 2012.

Civil, Marta, and R. Andrade. "Collaborative Practice with Parents: The Role of the Researcher as Mediator." In *Collaborations in Teacher Education: Examples from the Context of Mathematics Education*, edited by Andrea Peter-Koop, Vania Santos-Wagner, Chris Breen, and Andy Begg, 153–68. Boston, MA: Kluwer, 2003.

Common Core State Standards Initiative (CCSSI). *Common Core State Standards for Mathematics.* Washington, DC: National Governors Association Center for Best Practices and the Council of Chief State School Officers, 2010. http://www.corestandards.org/the-standards.

Dana, Nancy Fichtman. *Digging Deeper into Action Research: A Teacher Inquirer's Field Guide*. Thousand Oaks, CA: Corwin Press, 2013.

Epstein, Joyce. "Toward a Theory of Family-School Connections: Teacher Practices and Parental Involvement." In *Social Intervention: Potential and Constraints*, edited by Klaus Hurrelmann, Frederick Kaufmann, and Frederick Losel, 22–27. New York: DeGruyter, 1987.

Epstein, Joyce, and F. Van Voorhis. "School Counselors' Roles in Developing Partnerships with Families and Communities for Student Success." *Professional School Counseling* 14 (2010): 1–14.

Jeynes, W. H. "The Salience of the Subtle Aspects of Parental Involvement and Encouraging That Involvement: Implications for School-Based Programs." *Teachers College Record* 112 (2010): 747–74.

Remillard, J. T., and K. Jackson. "Old Math, New Math: Parents' Experiences with Standards Based Reform." *Mathematical Thinking and Learning* 8 (2006): 231–59.

Vukovic, R. K., S. O. Roberts, and L. G. Wright. "From Parental Involvement to Children's Mathematical Performance: The Role of Mathematics Anxiety." *Early Education and Development* 24 (2013): 446–67.

Walker, J., S. Shenker, and K. Hoover-Dempsey. "Why Do Parents Become Involved in Their Children's Education? Implications for School Counselors." *Professional School Counseling* 14 (2010): 27–41.

CHAPTER TWO

~

Surfacing Perspectives through Surveying

In this chapter, descriptions of how surveying can serve as a means for investigating parents' perspectives on their child's mathematics education are provided. Three field-tested surveys are included and coupled with teachers' findings and responsive action steps. In conclusion, questions are posed and suggestions offered for you to ponder while planning to survey at your school setting. Chapter-related resources for supporting parents through the grades with mathematics are shared as well.

> *Most of my parents view their role as only checking that their child's homework is done and reviewing for upcoming tests. Could this perspective exist because of me? Have I not actively engaged parents?*

> *Fourth-Grade Teacher, New York, New York*

The surveys shared with you in this chapter helped teachers surface parents' perspectives about (a) mathematics teaching and learning; (b) parents' role in that process; and (c) how teachers can support parents with mathematics. Three parent surveys adapted from those used by me, along with those teachers I have worked with over the years, are included in this chapter for your reference. Adaptations were made for purposes of clarity and did not impact upon the findings shared in this chapter (Mistretta 2008b; Mistretta 2012; Mistretta 2013a; Mistretta 2013b). The surveys can also be found at http://tinyurl.com/ltpw6af for your direct use or adaption.

Survey 1: Purpose

Survey 1 involves thirteen statements clustered into two categories. The first cluster, namely, Cluster 1, inquires about student comfort levels with mathematics as perceived by their parents; the second cluster, namely, Cluster 2, inquires about forms of teacher support parents desire concerning how to assist their child in learning mathematics. Specifically, Cluster 1 statements (#1–7) query parents' perceptions of their child's difficulties, if any, with mathematical concepts, computational skills, and problem solving; while Cluster 2 statements (#8–13) query parents' desire for support with (a) knowledge of current mathematics standards; (b) forms of mathematics assessment; and (c) ways to develop their child's mathematics conceptual understandings, computational fluencies, and problem-solving strategies. The last two items on the survey require narrative responses that call upon parents to share what it is like helping their children with mathematics, and the areas of mathematics they are interested in knowing more about.

Survey 1

After each statement, circle the number in each row that corresponds to your response.

   1=strongly disagree 2=disagree 3=uncertain 4=agree 5=strongly agree

1. My child often has difficulty learning mathematics concepts (meanings or ideas).

   1 2 3 4 5

2. My child often has difficulty using manipulatives (moveable objects) and/or pictures when learning mathematics.

   1 2 3 4 5

3. My child often has difficulty remembering basic addition, subtraction, multiplication, and/or division facts.

   1 2 3 4 5

4. My child often has difficulty completing a computation example (addition, subtraction, multiplication, and/or division).

   1 2 3 4 5

5. My child often has difficulty determining the unknown when problem solving.

      1   2   3   4   5

6. My child often has difficulty gathering necessary information when
   problem solving.

      1   2   3   4   5

7. My child often has difficulty developing a plan when problem
   solving.

      1   2   3   4   5

8. As a parent, I would like to know more about the current mathematics standards that guide my child's learning of mathematics.

      1   2   3   4   5

9. As a parent, I would like to know more about the components of
   the standardized mathematics tests.

      1   2   3   4   5

10. As a parent, I would like to know more about how my child's work
    is evaluated on standardized tests—that is, to understand the scoring
    rubric.

       1   2   3   4   5

11. As a parent, I would like to know more about how to help develop
    my child's mathematics conceptual understandings (meanings or
    ideas).

       1   2   3   4   5

12. As a parent, I would like to know more about how to help develop
    my child's computational fluencies (addition, subtraction, multipli-
    cation, and/or division).

       1   2   3   4   5

13. As a parent, I would like to know more about how to help develop
    my child's problem-solving strategies.

       1   2   3   4   5

14. Helping my child with math is . . .

15. I'd like to know more about . . .

Survey 1: Findings

When I began my inquiry journey about parents and mathematics twelve years ago, I distributed Survey 1 and received responses from a population of 790 parents of first- through eighth-grade children from ten schools in Queens, New York. All of these parents were of low socioeconomic status, with a child classified with low mathematics achievement levels. Their ethnic backgrounds were 7% Asian, 30% African American, 13% Caucasian, 46% Hispanic, and 4% Pacific Islander. For quantitative analysis purposes, parents' responses were categorized into two groups; namely, Group 1 and Group 2. Group 1 consisted of parents with a child in grades one through four, and represented 49% of the parents surveyed. Group 2 consisted of parents with a child in grades five through eight, and represented the remaining 51% of the parents surveyed. Data were input into Excel spreadsheets, and mean responses to individual survey statements were calculated. Independent samples t-tests concerning the overall mean responses were performed to note any significant differences ($p<.01$) among the parent groups.

It was determined that both parent groups were uncertain about the areas of mathematics that challenged their children. Both groups also tended to strongly agree they needed better knowledge of current mathematics standards, forms of assessment, and practical ways to help their children do mathematics at home.

It was interesting to note that the parents of children in grades one through four significantly agreed more to statements affirming their desire for ways to help their children develop conceptual understandings, computational fluency, and problem-solving strategies than the parents of children in grades five through eight. It was evident that middle school parents needed to better understand the critical role they play throughout their child's academic career.

Qualitative analysis processes, specifically *coding* and *memoing*, were used to surface emerging categories among the parents' narrative responses. Schwandt's (1997) *Qualitative Inquiry: A Dictionary of Terms* defines these processes as follows:

Coding
To begin the process of analyzing the large volume of data generated in the form of transcripts, field notes, photographs, and the like, the qualitative

inquirer engages in the activity of coding. Coding is a procedure that disaggregates that data, breaks it down into manageable segments and identifies or names those segments. . . . Coding requires constantly comparing and contrasting various successive segments of data and subsequently categorizing them. (p. 16)

Memoing
A procedure suggested by Barney Glaser (1978) for explaining or elaborating on the coded categories that the field-worker develops in analyzing data. Memos are conceptual in intent, vary in length, and are primarily written by oneself. The content of memos can include commentary on the meaning of a coded category, explanations of a sense of pattern developing among categories, a description of some specific aspect of a setting or phenomenon, and so forth. Typically, the final analysis and interpretation is based on integration and analysis of memos. (pp. 89–90)

Pleas for help emerged among both parent groups' narrative responses, representative comments being:

- "Math in our house is a nightmare. We need help!"
- "Multistep problem solving is a real PROBLEM."
- "I need answers to my child's questions about how mathematics applies to the real world."
- "The mathematics today is taught differently than in my time. I need help because I don't want to confuse my child."
- "We need to understand *both* the content and the methods of teaching it in order to help our children the right way."

Parents requested hands-on workshops to learn how to use the manipulatives (moveable objects) that their children were using in school. Parents asked for lists of software titles and online resources to help them "do mathematics together at home."

In addition, there was a significant amount of parents in both groups who felt insecure about their own knowledge of mathematics content. They wanted background information about the mathematics taught in school; parents needed support for doing that mathematics themselves so they could, in turn, productively support their child.

Survey 1: Responsive Action Steps

These findings helped me design initiatives for cultivating meaningful parental engagement in children's learning of mathematics. I crafted a series of family engagement sessions for the ten schools' family populations. These sessions promoted parents as the link between home and school, regardless of a child's grade level, that can (a) enhance mathematical learning; (b) heighten interest in mathematics; (c) build confidence in mathematical abilities; and (d) improve attitudes toward mathematics. At these sessions, parents and children collaborated on tasks involving grade-specific concepts, skills, and problem-solving strategies learned in school. Related assigned home tasks provided parents with entry points for engaging in mathematics with their children because the assignments required contributions from both parent and child.

Follow-up sessions offered a forum for families to gather, share solutions, and discuss diverse approaches to solving the home tasks. For a complete description of these family engagement sessions, follow-up sessions, and related tasks and materials, please refer to my 2008 book titled *Teachers Engaging Parents and Children in Mathematical Learning: Nurturing Productive Collaboration*, published by Rowman & Littlefield Education.

Survey 2: Purpose

I went on to facilitate family engagement sessions with other groups of parents and their children at seven inner-city pre–K through eighth-grade schools in Brooklyn, Queens, and Manhattan, New York, this time wondering about both the type and extent of parents' collaboration with their children's learning of mathematics. I administered Survey 2 to investigate parental behaviors such as:

- helping their child with mathematics homework
- helping their child prepare for mathematics tests
- communicating with their child about what is being learned in mathematics class
- discussing diverse approaches with their child for solving mathematics problems
- communicating with the teacher about their child's progress
- voicing their questions/concerns

One narrative response survey question queried parents on what it was like helping their child with mathematics.

Survey 2

After each statement, circle the number in each row that corresponds to your response.

1=almost never 2=seldom 3=about half 4=usually 5=almost always

1. I provide a quiet setting for my child to do his/her mathematics homework.

   1   2   3   4   5

2. I ask my child what he/she is doing in mathematics class.

   1   2   3   4   5

3. I help my child prepare for mathematics tests.

   1   2   3   4   5

4. I help my child correct his/her mistakes on mathematics tests.

   1   2   3   4   5

5. I check to see if my child finishes his/her mathematics homework.

   1   2   3   4   5

6. I check to see if my child's mathematics homework is correct.

   1   2   3   4   5

7. I help my child correct his/her mistakes on mathematics homework.

   1   2   3   4   5

8. I ask my child to explain how he/she arrives at his/her solutions to mathematics problems.

   1   2   3   4   5

9. I talk with my child about different approaches to solving mathematics problems.

   1   2   3   4   5

10. I point out to my child how mathematics is used in our everyday lives.

1   2   3   4   5

11. I communicate with my child's mathematics teacher about his/her progress.

1   2   3   4   5

12. I communicate with my child's mathematics teacher about my needs concerning my child's learning of mathematics.

1   2   3   4   5

13. Helping my child with mathematics is . . .

Survey 2: Findings

Some 977 parents among the seven schools completed Survey 2. All parents were of low socioeconomic status and had a child with a low mathematics achievement level. Their ethnic backgrounds were 3% Asian, 53% African American, 23% Caucasian, and 20% Hispanic. For analysis purposes, parent responses were categorized into three groups; namely, Group 1, Group 2, and Group 3. Group 1 consisted of parents with a child in grades pre–K through two, and represented 32% of the parents surveyed. Group 2 consisted of parents with a child in grades three through five, and represented 35% of the parents surveyed. Group 3 consisted of parents with a child in grades six through eight, and represented the remaining 33% of the parents surveyed.

The quantitative analysis procedures reflected those used for Survey 1. Overall responses indicated regular levels of engagement between parents and children in grades pre–K through five, and moderate levels in grades six through eight. Deeper analysis surfaced significantly less engagement among parents of children in grades three through five as compared with parents of children in grades pre–K through two. Significantly less engagement was again noted with parents of children in grades six through eight when compared with parents of children in grades three through five. Parents of children in grades pre–K through five most often checked to see if homework was finished, and gave less attention to checking on the accuracy of that homework. Parents of children in grades six through eight most often provided a quiet setting for their children to complete homework and paid even less attention to checking on the accuracy of the completed homework.

In addition, among all parent groups, the least time was spent talking with teachers about concerns they had about their child's learning of mathematics. Qualitative analysis procedures reflective of those used for Survey 1 were conducted for the narrative responses. Findings similar to those from Survey 1 were found. Parents wanted to help their child but were frustrated due to their lack of content knowledge and familiarity with current classroom learning environments.

Survey 2: Responsive Action Steps

The need for meaningful and consistent parent engagement across all grade levels was evident. Parents needed to better understand their role as active partners in their child's learning of mathematics. Therefore, the family engagement sessions previously mentioned were facilitated at these schools as well. These sessions emphasized parent responsibilities that go beyond just checking that homework is completed and providing a quiet environment for a child to work in. I also recognized that the goal of empowering parents lies in great part with school-based professional development initiatives. I therefore selected a single school located in Manhattan, New York, to pilot a professional development program. My intent was to strengthen how the teachers at this school supported parents with mathematics; to do this, I engaged them in teacher inquiry.

All seven mathematics teachers of the school investigated parent-child collaboration while working with families in their own classrooms. The term *parent-child collaboration* in mathematics is meant to refer to the manner in which a parent and child work together on mathematical tasks such as daily homework and projects. The teachers were prepared to facilitate their own family engagement sessions, and all 147 of the school's families (one child and at least one parent) attended these sessions. Families received incentives for their involvement that included home instructional materials, raffles, and gift cards. Dinner was also served prior to each session. The families' ethnic backgrounds were 82% Hispanic, 14% African American, 3% Caucasian, and 1% Asian. All families were of low socioeconomic status and had a child with a low achievement level in mathematics.

Part of the teachers' inquiry involved administering Survey 2. As with previously described findings, these teachers noted limited parent-child discussion about how answers were obtained. Most parents were just checking that homework was done and reviewing for upcoming tests.

The teachers wondered, though, if the parents' limited engagement was a consequence of they themselves unintentionally limiting what parents do with their children; this chapter's opening quote comes from one of these teachers.

All of the teachers at the school initially acknowledged the value of engaging parents, yet admitted their lack of confidence in parents' content knowledge. They stated, "We ask parents to do what we think they can do; for example, checking homework, reviewing for tests, and drilling multiplication tables." When analyzing parents' narrative responses, these teachers noted that their assumptions about parents lacking content knowledge *was* correct. The majority of parents *did* reference their lack of content knowledge, as well as their differing learning environments as students themselves.

It was evident, though, that these parents wanted to help, and they desired to know how they could best support their children. In response, the teachers facilitated family engagement sessions with their classroom families; however, this was new for them. Previously, these teachers communicated with parents about classroom learning only through written letters that focused on classroom procedures such as when homework was given and how grades were calculated.

Because of the teachers' interactions with families in their classrooms, every teacher noted the benefits of engaging families in mathematics tasks. A representative comment was, "These sessions provide opportunities for me to build parents' content knowledge *and* understanding of why I teach the way I do."

The teachers' survey findings helped frame the content discussed at the sessions. For example, due to the teachers noting limited conversation between parents and children about mathematical thinking, teachers decided to stress with parents the necessity to talk about mathematics at home. They prompted parents to have conversations with their child that probed how their child was approaching problems.

The teachers encouraged parents and children to share their differing methods of solution and compare/contrast them, rather than judge one method as superior to the other. This guidance gave parents and children opportunities to come to know about each other's way of thinking and, in turn, to deepen their understanding and support of one another.

Survey 3: Purpose

Building upon the work done with these previously described in-service teachers, I infused teacher inquiry into my mathematics methods coursework for pre-service teachers at the university where I currently teach. The involved pre-service teachers used multiple forms of inquiry while working with families, one being surveying, to become "in the know" about parent-child collaborations and practices for supporting their future classroom families. Survey 3 helped the pre-service teachers determine parental perspectives on (a) how parents should assist with their child's learning of mathematics (Section I) and (b) how teachers should support parents with their child's learning of mathematics (Section II).

Section I statements reflect those of Survey 2, while Section II statements help to investigate specific forms of support parents desire.

Survey 3

Section I

Parents choose among many ways to assist their child in their mathematical learning. CIRCLE one choice to tell how important each of these is for YOU to conduct WITH YOUR child.

1=not important 2=a little important 3=uncertain 4=important 5=very important

1. Provide a quiet setting for my child to do mathematics homework.

    1   2   3   4   5

2. Check to see if my child is finished with his/her mathematics homework.

    1   2   3   4   5

3. Help my child correct their mistakes on mathematics homework.

    1   2   3   4   5

4. Help my child prepare for mathematics tests.

    1   2   3   4   5

5. Help my child correct their mistakes on mathematics tests.

    1   2   3   4   5

6. Ask my child in-depth questions about what he/she is doing in mathematics.

    1   2   3   4   5

7. Point out to my child how mathematics is used in everyday life.

   1   2   3   4   5

8. Ask my child to explain to me how they arrive at their mathematics solutions.

   1   2   3   4   5

9. Talk with my child about different answers and/or approaches to solving mathematics problems.

   1   2   3   4   5

Section II

Teachers choose among many ways to involve their students' parents in their child's mathematical learning. CIRCLE one choice to tell how important each of these is for YOUR child's teacher to do to involve YOU in YOUR child's mathematical learning.

1=not important 2=a little important 3=uncertain 4=important 5=very important

1. Send communications home about my child's mathematical learning in terms that I can understand.

   1   2   3   4   5

2. Send home news about things happening at school concerning mathematical learning.

   1   2   3   4   5

3. Send home information about how mathematics report-card grades are earned.

   1   2   3   4   5

4. Send home information about the mathematics concepts/skills my child needs to learn each year.

   1   2   3   4   5

5. Provide ideas to help me check my child's mathematics homework.

   1   2   3   4   5

6. Provide ideas to help me prepare my child for a mathematics test.

   1   2   3   4   5

7. Contact me if my child is having problems with mathematics.
      1   2   3   4   5

8. Contact me if my child does well or improves in mathematics.
      1   2   3   4   5

9. Provide me with guidance on how to pose in-depth questions that allow my child to explain to me how they arrive at their mathematics solutions.
      1   2   3   4   5

10. Provide me with guidance on how to talk with my child about different ways to solve a mathematics problem.
       1   2   3   4   5

11. Provide me with ideas to help me point out to my child how mathematics is used in everyday life.
       1   2   3   4   5

Survey 3: Findings

Some 150 parents of third- through fifth-grade children among twelve schools in Staten Island, New York, completed Survey 3. Parents were of low socioeconomic status and had a child with a low mathematics achievement level. Their ethnic backgrounds were 30% Hispanic, 33% African American, 33% Caucasian, and 4% Asian. For quantitative analysis purposes, data was input into Excel spreadsheets and mean responses were calculated. In addition, highest and lowest quartiles for these mean responses were determined by dividing the range for each of the two survey categories by four (Fraenkel and Wallen 2009).

As with previously surveyed parent populations, these parents viewed themselves mostly in a passive role when assisting their child with mathematics. Of most importance for the parents was to provide quiet settings and check that homework was complete and accurate. Of least importance was for them to pose in-depth questions.

In addition, parents weren't interested in getting support for communicating with their child about thought processes while solving mathematics problems. It was clear that parents needed to better understand how communication about mathematical thinking is an essential part of supporting their child's completion of mathematics homework.

Survey 3: Responsive Action Steps

The pre-service teachers focused their attention on the lower level of priority parents gave to verbal communication. They informed parents that when they encourage their child to communicate about their thinking while solving mathematics problems, they as parents help their child gather, organize, and clarify their thoughts, habits that can significantly contribute to conceptual understandings in mathematics (Flores and Brittain 2003).

The pre-service teachers sought to enhance parent-child communication by engaging families in two particular tasks, namely, Today's Date and Which One Doesn't Belong? (Fuys and Welchman Tishler 1979). Due to the tasks' multiple solutions and/or methods of solution, conversations sparked among the families. It was encouraging for the pre-service teachers to witness families celebrating diverse ways of thinking about mathematics problems rather than judging one approach as superior to another.

Today's Date

This task involves representing the numeral of a date in multiple ways. It builds conceptual understanding of numbers and provides opportunities to communicate about multiple correct solutions, as well as multiple reasons for a single solution. It is applicable to any day of the year in classrooms of all grade levels, and can be used to represent multiple concepts or a particular topic being introduced, developed, or reviewed. One simply offers the statement, Today is _____.

For example, if the date is September 28th, the task is to represent 28 in as many ways as you can. Following are some sample family responses.

$20 + 8$	$32 - 4$
XXVIII	I have \$35 and spend \$7. How
$81 \div 9 + 19$	much do I have left?
$(5 \times 5) + 3$	$28/1$
$3x + 9 = 93$	2 tens 8 ones

Which One Doesn't Belong?

This task involves comparing and contrasting four examples to determine one example that differs from the others. A sample task and family responses follow.

$$18$$
$$+\ 14$$

$$6 + 4$$

$$8$$
$$+\ 4$$

$$16$$
$$-\ 9$$

Figure 2.1.

Family responses:

- 18 + 14 because it is the only example where both numbers contain double digits
- 6 + 4 because it is the only example that is written horizontally
- 16 – 9 because it is the only example without a 4 in it
- 16 – 9 because it is the only example that has a prime answer
- 8 + 4 because it is the only example that contains one numeral that is half the other

Related curriculum skills include sorting and classification, both of which are early algebraic reasoning skills. Tasks can reflect current classroom topics, and families can also be given blank templates to create their own task.

Planning Your Survey Inquiry

- As previously stated, surveying can help investigate parents' perspectives on mathematics teaching and learning, as well as the extent to which parents and children work together in mathematics.
  - What perspectives and forms of parent-child collaboration do you wonder about?
  - What findings shared in this chapter would you like to further investigate with your classroom parents?
  - How might you use/adapt a survey(s) shared in this chapter to help answer your question(s)?
- The surveys shared in this chapter surfaced parents' (a) insecurity in their own content knowledge; (b) unfamiliarity with current methods

of teaching mathematics; (c) passive forms of involvement; and
(d) decreasing levels of engagement as grade levels heightened.

- ◆ How would you respond to parents' insecurity with their own
  content knowledge?
- ◆ How would you respond to parents' unfamiliarity with current
  methods of teaching mathematics?
- ◆ How would you respond to parents' passive forms of
  involvement?
- ◆ How would you respond to parents' low level of engagement in
  middle/high school grade levels?

- Once you have collected data through surveying, your analysis of that
  survey data begins. For quantitative data, calculate mean responses to
  individual survey statements and/or clusters of statements as was previously explained in this chapter. For qualitative data, begin by simply
  reading through your narrative responses once or twice.

  Ask yourself the following questions, adapted from those crafted by
  Nancy Fichtman Dana (2013) to start making sense of your quantitative and qualitative data.

  - ◆ Why did I collect this data about parents in the first place?
  - ◆ What do I notice about the data I collected about parents?
  - ◆ How would I describe to others the data I collected about
    parents?

- For your qualitative data analysis, engage in the coding and memoing
  that was previously defined in this chapter. To help in determining
  codes for your data, ask yourself the following questions, adapted from
  those crafted by Nancy Fichtman Dana (2013).

  - ◆ What is most interesting about the data I gathered about
    parents?
  - ◆ What are some things in my data about parents that stand out
    from the rest?
  - ◆ How might I fit different pieces of my data about parents
    together?

- Once your data analysis is complete, you can tell a story about what
  you came to know about parents and mathematics. Reflect now on
  these following questions, again adapted from the work of Nancy
  Fichtman Dana (2013), as you craft your story.

  - ◆ What have I learned about my classroom parents through
    surveying?
  - ◆ What implications do my findings have on my practices con-
    cerning parents?

- What changes might I make in how I support parents?
- What new wonderings do I have now about parents and mathematics as a result of surveying?

Supporting Parents through the Grades

The parents described in this chapter requested (a) content information; (b) online resources; (c) strategies for helping with homework; and (d) ways to communicate with their child about mathematics. Across all grade levels, Khan Academy (www.khanacademy.org) can support parents' content knowledge. Mobile apps are available from the National Council of Teachers of Mathematics at http://illuminations.nctm.org/content.aspx?id=3855. In addition, this organization's website contains interactive online resources families can use according to grade-level bands listed below.

Pre–K through Grade Two
- http://illuminations.nctm.org/Search.aspx?view=search&type=ac&gr=Pre-K-2

Grades Three through Five
- http://illuminations.nctm.org/Search.aspx?view=search&type=ac&gr=3-5

Grades Six through Eight
- http://illuminations.nctm.org/Search.aspx?view=search&type=ac&gr=6-8

Grades Nine through Twelve
- http://illuminations.nctm.org/Search.aspx?view=search&type=ac&gr=9-12

Homework tips across grade levels can be found on this website at http://www.nctm.org/resources/content.aspx?id=2147483782. These tips emphasize parents' role as "guide on the side" as opposed to "sage on the stage." The following list of questions for parents to pose while working with their child supports parents in their role as guide at all grade levels. These questions are those recommended by the National Council of Teachers of Mathematics (NCTM 2000).

- What is the problem you're working on?
- What do the directions say?
- What words or directions do you not understand?
- Where do you think you should begin?
- What do you already know that can help you work through the problem?
- What have you done so far?
- Do you have similar problems to look at?
- Can you draw a picture or make a diagram?
- Can you explain what the teacher asked us to do?
- Can you tell me where you are stuck?
- Can we use another approach to arrive at the same solution?
- Is there another solution to this problem? Why or why not?

The teachers described in this chapter found that the task Which One Doesn't Belong? enhanced the emotional quality of parent-child interaction because of its multiple approaches and/or multiple solutions. This task reduced the anxieties that can form when determining only one correct answer, or only one correct way of arriving at that answer. Shared below are additional examples of the task for your use with families at different grade-level bands. Although the examples are categorized, each of them can be used to compare/contrast the appearance of examples for the purpose of supporting mathematical reasoning at all grade levels. These tasks can also be found at http://tinyurl.com/ltpw6af for your direct use and/or adaption.

Pre-K through Grade Two

Figure 2.2. Which One Doesn't Belong?

```
   29                    9
  +14                   +4
  ————                  ——

    7                   18
   +4                   - 9
  ————                  ——
```

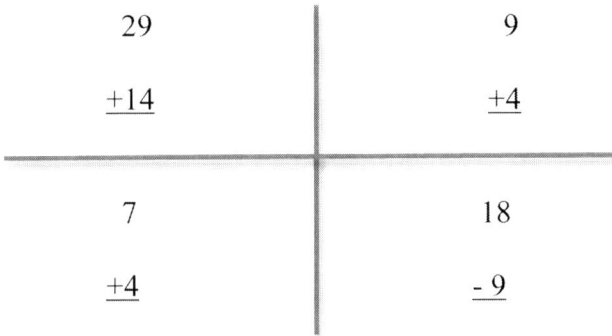

Figure 2.3. Which One Doesn't Belong?

Grades Three through Five

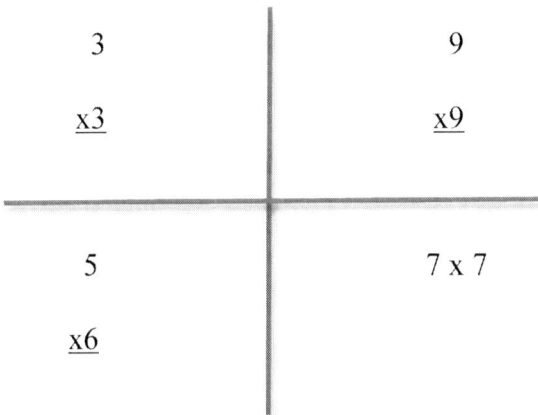

```
    3                    9
   x3                   x9
  ————                  ——

    5                 7 x 7
   x6
  ————
```

Figure 2.4. Which One Doesn't Belong?

$\dfrac{50}{100}$	$\dfrac{5}{10}$
.05	$\dfrac{1}{2}$

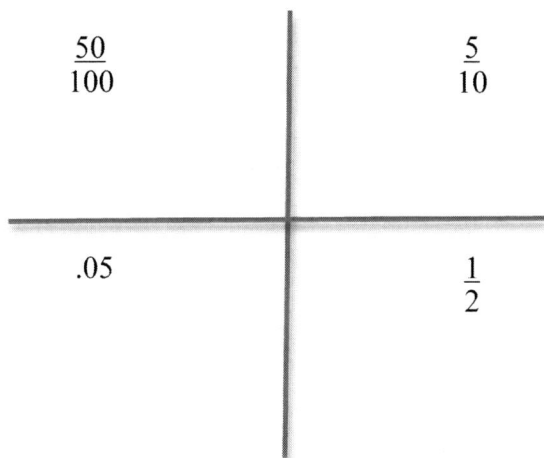

Figure 2.5. Which One Doesn't Belong?

Grades Six through Eight

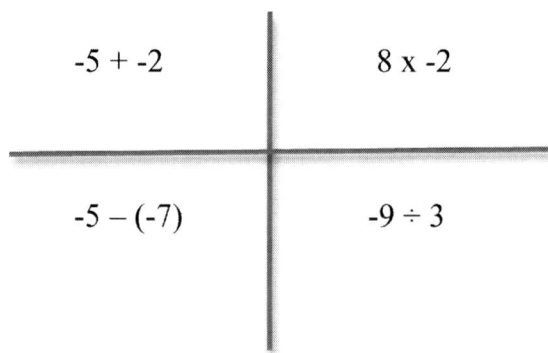

-5 + -2	8 x -2
-5 − (-7)	-9 ÷ 3

Figure 2.6. Which One Doesn't Belong?

$$\frac{2r + 6}{5} = -4 \qquad \qquad 10 = x/3 + x/7$$

$$.5x - .3x = 8 \qquad \qquad x^2 + x = 12$$

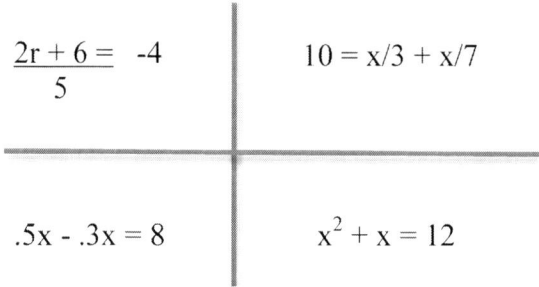

Figure 2.7. Which One Doesn't Belong?

The blank template below is for family members to use while making up their own Which One Doesn't Belong? to share with each other at home as well as at school gatherings.

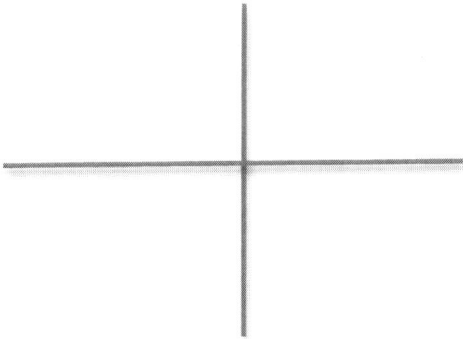

Figure 2.8. Which One Doesn't Belong?

References

Dana, Nancy Fichtman. *Digging Deeper into Action Research: A Teacher Inquirer's Field Guide.* Thousand Oaks, CA: Corwin Press, 2013.

Dana, Nancy Fichtman, and D. Yendol-Hoppey. *The Reflective Educator's Guide to Classroom Research.* Thousand Oaks, CA: Corwin Press, 2009.

Flores, A., and C. Brittain. "Writing to Reflect in a Mathematics Methods Course." *Teaching Children Mathematics* 10 (2003): 112–18.

Fraenkel, J. R., and N. E. Wallen. *How to Design and Evaluate Research in Education.* New York: McGraw-Hill, 2009.

Fuys, D., and R. Welchman Tishler. *Teaching Mathematics in the Elementary School.* New York: Harper Collins, 1979.

Glaser, B. G. *Theoretical Sensitivity Advances in the Methodology of Grounded Theory.* Mill Valley, CA: Sociology Press, 1978.

Mistretta, R. M. "Cultivating Parent-Child Collaboration Concerning Mathematical Learning: A Necessary Objective for Teacher Preparation Programs. In *Teacher Education Yearbook XVI: Imagining a Renaissance in Teacher Education*, edited by C. J. Craig and L. F. Deretchin, 348–62. Lanham, MD: Rowman & Littlefield Education, 2008a.

Mistretta, R. M. *Teachers Engaging Parents in Mathematical Learning: Nurturing Productive Collaboration.* Lanham, MD: Rowman & Littlefield Education, 2008b.

Mistretta, R. M. "Preparing Teachers to Cultivate Parent-Child Collaboration in Mathematics." *Journal of Mathematics Education Leadership* 14, no. 1 (2012): 63–71.

Mistretta, R. M. "Becoming 'In the Know' about Parent-Child Collaborations in Mathematics." *Mathematics Teacher Educator* 1, no. 2 (2013a): 5–15.

Mistretta, R. M. "'We Do Care,' Say Parents." *Teaching Children Mathematics* 19, no. 9 (2013b): 572–80.

National Council of Teachers of Mathematics (NCTM). *Principles and Standards for School Mathematics.* Reston, VA: NCTM, 2000.

Schwandt, T. A. *Qualitative Inquiry: A Dictionary of Terms.* Thousand Oaks, CA: Sage Publications, Inc., 1997.

CHAPTER THREE

~

Witnessing Parent-Child Interactions through Observation

In this chapter, observation is described as a means for witnessing how parents and children work together on mathematical tasks. Forms of parent-child interaction to note while observing are explained, and coupled with teachers' findings and responsive action steps. In conclusion, questions and suggestions are offered for you to ponder while planning to observe at your school setting. Chapter-related resources for supporting parents through the grades with mathematics are shared as well.

> *Parental styles of assistance are so diverse. I've watched parents who hesitate to help their children because they doubt their own math skills. Then there are those parents who are really good in math; however, their assistance can take one of two directions. They either patiently guide their child's thinking by posing good questions, or become so frustrated when their child doesn't understand that they cause really tense and unproductive conditions between themselves and their child.*
>
> *Fifth-Grade Teacher, Staten Island, New York*

Observing parents and children while they work together on mathematical tasks offers teachers opportunities to witness behaviors. For example, teachers can note parents' level of engagement, and the types of questions they pose. Teachers can also observe how parents approach problems, as well as parents' reactions when their child's approach differs from their own.

Parents do care, and they want to help their child. However, parents come to the academic table with different skill sets and needs (Mellon and Moutavelis 2011; Civil, Díez-Palomar, Menéndez-Gómez, and Acosta-Iriqui

2008); and observation is an inquiry approach teachers can use to determine how best to support parents' diverse circumstances. Following are steps to take prior to, during, and after observing parent-child interactions.

Determining What to Observe

The first step is to determine the direction to take for your observation. You can decide to see what unfolds as parents and children interact; or you may want to observe specific behaviors. Observations might serve to answer a question(s) stemming from your survey findings.

Teachers this author has worked with wondered about (a) the general quality of parent-child communication, and (b) the types of questions parents pose to their children when working on mathematical tasks together. These teachers used the following questions to guide their observations of parents and children working together on mathematics problems.

- Are parents positive or negative in tone when communicating with their child?
- How are parents explaining to their child and/or exploring ideas?
- What short answer, prompting, and/or probing questions are parents posing to their child?

Gathering Families

Once you determine your purpose for observing families, the logistics behind gathering those families in order to observe them needs to be addressed. To maximize parents' attendance, consider parents' preferences in gathering times, and announce gatherings early enough for parents to make arrangements to attend.

Sending an invitation that informs parents of a gathering's intent and inquires about times that best suit their schedules creates a feeling of consideration and real partnership (De La Cruz 1999). You can then review responses and determine the most appropriate meeting time(s).

Wording for an Invitation, Query Form, Announcement, and related Response Form used by teachers I have worked with are shared below. The documents can be found at http://tinyurl.com/ltpw6af for your direct use or adaption.

Invitation

The invitation informed parents of their importance in their child's mathematics education, as well as the teacher's intention to tailor support for parents in their role as academic partner.

Dear Parents,

You are your child's academic partners at home who can positively influence their attitudes and achievement, especially in mathematics. You are an intellectual resource to me as well; for when home and school are connected, optimal conditions exist for student achievement.

My intent is to support you to the best of my ability in your role as academic partner. To do this, I am hosting a Family Mathematics Gathering for parent(s) and their child(ren) so as to observe how you and your child(ren) work together on mathematical tasks. Your participation will allow me to better understand how I can tailor my support of your efforts to assist your child at home with mathematics.

This gathering will be held for one hour and scheduled with consideration of the busy schedules of all those involved. Therefore, please indicate on the attached query form the day and time you prefer.

I look forward to partnering with you in the most productive ways.

Sincerely,

To personalize the experience, students can design their own cover for their parent invitation. This can be an exciting task for children because they can put their personal touch on an event planned for both them and their parents. Parents, in turn, are invited by both their child and their child's teacher, conveying to parents that they are an important and welcomed part of their child's academic life.

Figure 3.1.

Query Form

The text of the following query form serves to determine the most appropriate gathering times for parents. The query form also serves as an organizational tool. The names of both children and their attending family members need to be indicated on the form, which helps with record keeping.

Please return this query form by _____.

Circle the most appropriate time for you and your child to attend a Family Mathematics Gathering.

Weeknight beginning at 7PM (Specify night) _____
Weeknight beginning at 8PM (Specify night) _____
Saturday morning beginning at 10AM _____
Saturday afternoon beginning at 1PM_____
Sunday morning beginning at 10AM _____
Sunday afternoon beginning at 1PM_____

Announcement

Following is an announcement that informs parents of the gathering, its purpose, and day/time based on the responses received. To maximize parents' attendance at gatherings, you, in consultation with your administrator, can consider one or a combination of the following incentives:

- pizza / ice cream parties in classrooms where all families attend
- raffles
- dinner
- instructional materials for families who attend

Dear Parents,

To best support your efforts to assist your child at home with mathematics, the Family Mathematics Gathering has been planned for you and your child. Your feedback concerning the most appropriate days and times for this gathering were carefully considered, and the following date and time reflects common responses.

[insert date and time]

As noted in previous correspondence, this gathering allows me to observe how you and your child work together on mathematics tasks. In turn I will come to know how best to tailor my support of you as academic partner to both your child and your child's school. By connecting home and school, we provide optimal conditions for your child's mathematics achievement.

I look forward to partnering with you.

Sincerely,

Response Form
Parents are given the opportunity on the following response form to indicate reasons why they might not be able to participate. Knowing such reasons allows for accommodations to be made where possible. We can't assume that parents' lack of participation is due to lack of interest. There may be very good reasons that, when known, can be remedied.

Please return this response form by _____ .

We (will, will not) attend the Family Mathematics Gathering.

If you will not attend, please explain why on the back of this form so I can try to partner with you in another way.

Name of Parent(s) Attending _____
_____

Name of Child(ren) Attending _____
_____
_____

Parent(s) Signature(s):
_____
_____

Student(s) Signature(s):
_____
_____

Engaging Families

Next consider how to engage families so as to capture the interactions you wonder about. Some teachers I have worked with engaged their fourth- and fifth-grade families in solving the Tupelo Township Problem (found at http://www.wmich.edu/math/m2rap/TupeloTownshipRevised.pdf) or tasks from the grades one through eight *Roads to Reasoning* series, published by Creative Publications, to witness how families interacted when solving word problems together.

Other teachers observed how parents and children used manipulatives (moveable objects) such as tangrams, pattern blocks, and Cuisenaire rods to represent mathematical concepts and procedures. Still others wanted to see how parents and children reacted to tasks involving multiple solutions. These teachers engaged families in the Today's Date and Which One Doesn't Belong? tasks previously described in chapter 2.

Taking Field Notes

While observing, you need to take field notes to document what you witness. Field notes are not explanations, but rather focus on keeping a record of what is occurring without commenting on the reasons for the behaviors, or judging them. These notes are data to reflect on after your observation is completed.

Teachers I have worked with took field notes in a variety of ways such as scripting conversation, noting what a parent and child were doing at particular time intervals, and recording specific questions parents posed to their child as they worked through mathematical tasks. Using a template such as the one provided below helped organize what they saw. This template can also be found at http://tinyurl.com/ltpw6af for your direct use or adaption.

Family Observed:		
Parent Behavior	*Evidence*	*Child Reaction*
General Attitude • positive ( ) • negative ( ) Posing Questions • short answer ( ) • prompting ( ) • probing ( ) • extending ( )		

Figure 3.2.

Family Observed:		
Parent Behavior	*Evidence*	*Child Reaction*
Eliciting child's ideas/ thinking strategies		
Discussing different approaches		
Treating errors or strategies that didn't work as opportunities for learning		
Highlighting connections among involved mathematics topics		
Highlighting applications of involved mathematics topics		

Figure 3.2. (continued)

To provide conditions for capturing as many interactions as possible, as well as confirming your own observations, have colleagues join you in taking these field notes. Conference beforehand so that everyone who joins you (a) understands the purpose of the observation; (b) focuses on the parent-child interactions you have chosen to investigate; and (c) uses the same procedure for taking field notes.

You might also consider having colleagues videotape as a means for capturing parent-child interactions. Using video can help gather descriptive information and better capture and understand behavior progressions. More specifically, attitudes, skills, knowledge levels, types of interactions, and nonverbal behavior can be observed in videos (Cloutier et al. 1987) and later transcribed.

However, this option, although an extremely powerful form of data collection, may not be conducive to all families acting as naturally as they would without the video camera present. So although videoing is optimal, realize you may need to couple it, or even replace it, with taking field notes as previously explained.

Findings and Responsive Action Steps
The findings shared in this section stem from teachers' observations of over three hundred families and analysis of their field notes reflected the qualitative methods described in chapter 2. Teachers found that most parents took

control of conversations in an explanatory manner, using only one method of solution (their own), and only posing short-answer questions that required a yes/no or single number response from their child.

Some parents guided their child's thought processes, while others caused tension to exist between themselves and their child. For example, a fourth-grade teacher witnessed a father so frustrated with his child's lack of understanding that he just "took over" in an abrupt manner, causing the child to "freeze up and tune out."

Based on what the teachers observed, they became aware of the need to cultivate better conditions for communication between parents and children where both parent and child could learn from each other. To work toward such a goal, the teachers facilitated Family Engagement Sessions reflective of those described in chapter 2, and families were gathered through invitations and follow-up announcements similar to those described previously in this chapter.

Families were strategically grouped together so that parents observed by teachers as demonstrating negative forms of assistance were grouped with parents the teachers observed as working more productively with their child. Time was allotted at the sessions for parents to discuss their approaches, share challenges, and offer advice to each other. Parents were also guided to pose the supportive questions listed in chapter 2 while working on tasks with their child as a means for cultivating collaborative and insightful conversations among family members.

Encouraging moments occurred for the teachers when they witnessed parents shifting their role at these sessions from telling to listening and guiding. Parents were receptive to teachers' guidance; they appeared to enjoy talking with their children about their mathematical thinking, and they welcomed conversation with other families about challenges and practical advice.

Teachers were also excited to see the children gaining confidence and "stepping up" to explain and make their thinking visible to their parents. A third-grade teacher stated, "Because I saw how proud my students were to explain their work to their parents, I realize even more now how critical it is to communicate with parents about how to interact with their kids during homework time."

This particular teaching began by (a) promoting family conversations by assigning home tasks involving multiple approaches and/or solutions; (b) inviting parents to sit in on a class or two during the school day; and (c) posting online classroom footage of her lessons (with appropriate permissions).

Teachers also used their observation findings to support families during individual report-card conferences. Some teachers discussed their general findings with parents at school meetings and distributed responsive materials. Others assigned collaborative parent-child homework using the Today's Date and Which One Doesn't Belong? tasks described in chapter 2.

Another responsive action step was to host what teachers called Coffee, Cake, and Conversation gatherings for small groups of parents either before school started or in the evening. Because of the rich conversations they observed among parents during the family engagement sessions, they wanted to provide conditions for parents to expand upon the conversations they started.

Such gatherings promoted a supportive learning community. Parents became aware of challenges they shared, in turn feeling less isolated from each other. Parents with children in multiple grades gave helpful feedback about domain progressions and the mathematical practices of the Common Core State Standards for Mathematics. For example, one parent with children in third and sixth grade shared with her group how she noticed connections among the content standards and mathematical practices through the grades.

Witnessing how classroom families worked together informed teachers' responsive action steps. This can be the case for you as well when you observe what unfolds as your classroom families collaborate on the mathematical tasks you engage them in.

Planning Your Observation Inquiry

Guidance for planning your own observations of families working together on mathematics tasks have permeated throughout this chapter's content thus far. This section builds upon that guidance and focuses your lens on your specific wonderings.

- Observing parent-child interactions allows you to witness what parents do well, as well as those areas where parents need your support.
  - What aspects of how parents and children interact while working on mathematical tasks do you wonder about?
  - How will you plan to witness those behaviors?
  - How do you plan to process what you witness so as to appropriately respond to your findings?
- While observing parent-child interactions, teachers described in this chapter noted varying forms of parental assistance. Some parents guided their children's thought processes, while others took charge and caused tension between themselves and their child.

- ◆ How would you respond if you note parents assisting their child in a productive manner?
- ◆ How would you respond if you note parents assisting their child in a nonproductive manner?
- As stated previously, collecting and analyzing data allows you to tell a story. Once you have collected your observation data, your analysis of that data begins. As recommended in chapter 2, take your field notes and simply read through them once or twice. Use those same questions included in chapter 2 to start making sense of the parent-child interactions you witnessed.
  - ◆ Why did I collect this data about parents in the first place?
  - ◆ What do I notice about the data I collected about parents?
  - ◆ How would I describe the data I collected about parents to others?
- Engage in coding and memoing your data, again using more of those questions included in chapter 2.
  - ◆ What is most interesting about the data I have about parents?
  - ◆ What are some things in my data about parents that stand out from the rest?
  - ◆ How might I fit together different pieces of my data about parents?
- Once your observation data analysis is complete, you can tell a story about what you came to know about parents. Reflect now on still more questions that were indicated in chapter 2 with a lens now focused on your observation data.
  - ◆ What have I learned about my classroom parents through observing?
  - ◆ What implications do my findings have on my practices concerning parents?
  - ◆ What changes might I make in how I support parents?
  - ◆ What new wonderings do I have now about parents and mathematics as a result of observing?

Supporting Parents through the Grades

As stated previously, the supportive questions teachers provided to parents to pose while working with their child on mathematics tasks were extremely helpful. The following link lists those questions, along with others that help cultivate productive conversation between parents and children through the grades.

http://www.nctm.org/resources/content.aspx?id=2876

Additional related family resources provided by the National Council of Teachers of Mathematics that are relevant for all grade levels can be accessed using the link http://www.nctm.org/resources/families.aspx. These resources are titled:

- Help Your Child Succeed in Math
- Math Education Today

A child benefits when his parent supports his mathematical learning at home in a manner that reflects classroom learning. One way to show parents what classroom mathematics learning environments look like is to invite them to visit your classroom during a mathematics lesson. A teacher previously mentioned in this chapter videoed lessons and posted them online for parents to view on the school's secured website. If your school conditions prevent such an action step, another option is to share other classroom footage available online to the public.

Listed below are links to classroom videos across grade-level bands that portray the teaching of the Common Core State Standards for Mathematics and their Mathematical Practices. You can select videos for parents to watch according to specific mathematics content domains as a means for developing parents' familiarity with current mathematics teaching and learning environments.

Kindergarten through Grade Four
- http://learner.org/resources/series32.html

Grades Five through Eight
- http://learner.org/resources/series33.html

Grades Nine through Twelve
- http://learner.org/resources/series34.html

References

Civil, M., J. Díez-Palomar, J. M. Menéndez-Gómez, and J. Acosta-Iriqui. "Parents' Interactions with their Children When Doing Mathematics." Paper presented at the Annual Meeting of the American Educational Research Association (AERA), New York, NY, March 2008.

Cloutier, D., B. Lilley, D. Phillips, B. Weber, and D. Sanderson. *A Guide to Program Evaluation and Reporting.* Orono, ME: University of Maine Cooperative Extension Service, 1987.

De La Cruz, Y. "Reversing the Trend: Latino Families in Real Partnerships with Schools." *Teaching Children Mathematics* 5, no. 5 (1999): 296–300.

Gal, I., and A. Stoudt. *Family Achievement in Mathematics.* NCAL Connections. Philadelphia: National Center on Adult Literacy, University of Pennsylvania, 1995.

Mellon, R. C., and A. G. Moutavelis. "Parental Educational Practices in Relation to Children's Anxiety Disorder-Related Behavior." *Journal of Anxiety Disorders* 25 (2011): 829–34. doi: 10.1016/j.janxdis.2011.04.003.

National Council of Teachers of Mathematics (NCTM). *Principles and Standards for School Mathematics.* Reston, VA: NCTM, 2000.

Sheldon, S. B., and J. L. Epstein. "Involvement Counts: Family and Community Partnerships and Math Achievement." *Journal of Educational Research* 98, no. 4 (2005): 196–206.

CHAPTER FOUR

~

Digging Deeper through Interviewing

In this chapter, interviewing is explained as a means for deepening what you have come to know about parents and mathematics. Questions to ask during interviews are included, coupled with teachers' findings and responsive action steps. In conclusion, questions are posed and suggestions offered for you to ponder while planning to interview at your school setting. Chapter-related resources for supporting parents through the grades with mathematics are shared as well.

> *My classroom parents really do care, and want to be involved in the learning process. However, I learned through conversations with some of my parents that they work late, and by the time they arrive home they don't have enough time to go over homework in a way they would like to. This made me realize I need to create manageable conditions for parents to interact with their children on projects.*
>
> *Second-Grade Teacher, New York, New York*

Interviewing, in this chapter, refers to informal conversations with parents and children. This inquiry approach shares the same ultimate goal as surveying and observing—to know how to support parents with mathematics in ways that are tailored to families' specific circumstances.

Surveying, as discussed in chapter 2, is useful for surfacing parents' perspectives on mathematics teaching and learning, and a parent's role in that process. Observation, as discussed in chapter 3, is useful for witnessing parent and child behaviors while working together on mathematical tasks.

Interviewing, the focus of this chapter, can help confirm, clarify, as well as deepen findings acquired through surveying and observing.

Analyzing findings from such multiple data sources is known as "triangulation" (Cresswell 1998; Patton 2002) and allows the teacher inquirer to obtain a complete and accurate picture of what is being investigated. For example, a teacher, after reviewing her survey results, noted low ratings from parents for statements about (a) posing in-depth questions to children about mathematical thinking, and (b) pointing out real-world applications of mathematics to children. This teacher wondered why these statements received such low ratings.

Through interviewing, she came to understand that the parents who responded with these low ratings weren't confident in their own mathematics content knowledge. Several of these parents also weren't aware themselves about how mathematics connects with everyday life other than for business purposes. During interviews with these parents, they explained how challenging it was for them as parents to apply mathematics for their children beyond what they were taught in school. Upon coming to know about the challenges these parents were facing, the teacher set out to (a) nurture parents' confidence in themselves as academic partners to their child, and (b) promote parents' awareness of how everyday life connects with mathematics. She stated:

> I understand that many parents may not feel they have the content base to help their child. However, a lack of content knowledge doesn't have to be a barrier. When parents provide opportunities for their child to just talk about what they know about a problem, and how they are thinking about solving it, they help their child organize and clarify their thoughts. Parents can even help their child form questions to ask me in the classroom. I need to let parents know how helpful it is when they guide their child to think through a mathematics problem by posing good questions.

Interviewing also allows teachers to spontaneously pose additional questions they might not have even considered posing prior to an interview or on a survey. Such opportunities to probe into parents' responses can uncover "back stories" that inform teachers' responsive action steps. This chapter's opening quote is an example of a teacher who found herself in such a position.

During an interview with one of her second-grade families, she came to know that, although the parents wanted to work with their child on projects, time was limited. A middle school teacher had a similar experience. He stated, "One parent I spoke to works two jobs, arrives home at midnight, and wakes up at 5 a.m. to check that his son's homework is correct before going to work the next day."

These teachers learned not to assume that busy parents are not involved parents. Rather, teachers need to create conditions, such as manageable amounts of time for families to work together on projects. Teachers also need to reflect on how family projects can support the quality of time that parents and children spend together. As a middle school parent stated, "I do not get too much time to spend with my child. So, I'd rather be involved in something more entertaining than doing traditional workbook pages together."

Such a comment sparked a teacher to consider family projects that involved excursions such as visiting MoMath, a hands-on mathematics museum in New York City. Hunting for shapes in one's neighborhood was another idea for a family project, as well as looking for mathematics while cooking and finding the best buys at one's local supermarket.

Conducting Interviews

Interviews can be conducted with individual parents/families, or with groups of parents/families. The choices you make depend on what you want to investigate. Once those decisions are made, ensure that the interview setting is free from distractions so participants can concentrate on the matter at hand.

Take field notes, as described in chapter 3, to document what you hear. Audio- or videotaping interviews, and later transcribing field notes, is optimal. However, taping or writing field notes during interviews can, at times, cause the conversation to flow less smoothly. Participants may not feel as comfortable speaking to you as they would without the equipment, or without you taking notes while they are speaking. If you find yourself in these types of situations, take notes as best you can, and sit yourself down immediately after the interview to write down the details of your conversation. This way your interview can flow as smoothly as possible, and you can document its content while it is still fresh in your mind.

Questions to Pose
The questions that follow were posed to parents by the pre-service and in-service teachers described in chapters 2 and 3, as well as New York City teaching fellows I worked with while on their journey toward knowing and supporting parents with mathematics. These teacher inquirers were seeking to clarify and/or expand upon parents' survey response(s), and/or investigate

the rationale for specific forms of parent-child interaction they noted during observations.

- Explain what you mean by . . .
- Can you give an example of . . .
- Can you describe in more detail . . .
- Why did you choose that approach to . . .

Teachers who were seeking to gather data to compare/contrast with survey and/or observation data posed the following questions to parents:

- What is your role in your child's learning of mathematics?
- What is your teacher's role in supporting you with your child's learning of mathematics?
- Does anything challenge you as a parent concerning your child's learning of mathematics?

Teachers who were seeking to investigate parents' reactions to school events, such as the family engagement sessions explained in previous chapters, stated to parents:

- Help me plan to support you in the future. Is there anything I should keep doing and why? Is there anything I should change and why? Is there anything I should stop doing and why?

Teachers who were seeking to investigate families' reactions to home tasks they assigned posed the following question to parents and children:

- How did it feel to work together on the mathematics task?

When hosting Coffee, Cake, and Conversation focus groups with parents, as discussed in chapter 3, the conversations started with teachers simply stating to parents:

- Describe your experiences helping your child with mathematics.

Sometimes school conditions may not lend themselves to posing the types of questions stated above in a face-to-face setting. Such circumstances, though, should not marginalize your opportunities to acquire the details these questions can elicit; these details ultimately inform how you can best support your classroom parents. If you find interviews challenging to conduct at your school, consider crafting a questionnaire to send home for parents to complete and return to you.

You might also consider asking parents to complete a questionnaire at the beginning of a general school meeting, or pose one or two questions at a parent-teacher conference. Still another option is to make the questionnaire available online with the use of online resources such as Survey Monkey (www.surveymonkey.com); this online option can also increase the return rate on the surveys discussed in chapter 1.

Findings and Responsive Action Steps

Teachers' analysis of their field notes from the interviews previously described reflected the qualitative methods described in chapter 2. Their findings and responsive action steps are organized below according to categories that emerged during data analysis; namely, unfamiliarity, receptiveness, and behaviors.

Unfamiliarity

As noted in previous chapters, parents' lack of mathematics content knowledge surfaced over and over again, as well as their strangeness to the manner in which mathematics is currently taught. Representative comments from parents were: "Mathematics today is taught differently than in my time. I want to help; however, I don't want to confuse my child," and "My struggle with early grades is the new methods; I'm a 'carry the one type.'"

Parents requested explanations on how to solve homework examples and "easy-to-navigate" directions on how to help their child. An eighth-grade parent stated, "Let me know the areas my child struggles with the most so I know what's most important to focus on." Parents also asked that teachers require students to take thorough notes in school as a means for communicating classroom content and expectations to parents at home. In addition, parents wanted curriculum guides and summaries of content.

In response, teachers shared with parents the grade-level priorities and key fluencies included in chapter 1. Teachers also began to include, with at least one homework example, an explanation of how to solve it. Another teacher response was to post detailed solutions to homework problems for parents to review online. Teachers did realize this might open the door to their students looking at the answers before/instead of trying to arrive at answers themselves. The behavior was discouraged by randomly calling on students the next day to explain answers as a way to confirm students' understanding of the material.

Teachers also recommended online resources to parents such as IXL (www .ixl.com) and Khan Academy (www.khanacademy.org). Since parents may be unfamiliar with the characteristics of educationally appropriate websites, recommending such online resources was helpful. As a parent of a middle and high school student pointed out, "It's difficult for me to search for additional resources online. So much is out there, and I don't know which to pick."

Still other teachers sent home manipulatives. They found that parents were unfamiliar with these instructional tools, and they wanted parents to have access to them. Paper versions of the manipulatives being used in school were sent home with explanations of their use and related home tasks for parents to engage in with their child.

These types of responsive action steps exemplify essential and meaningful teacher support for parents that build both content and pedagogical knowledge. Equally valuable, though, is teachers' support of parents' confidence in themselves as academic partners. A teacher stated, "I do not think parents' unfamiliarity with academic content is such a detriment. The two biggest areas parents can help their child with are focus and accountability. A lot of the time, it is not that students are completely clueless as to what to do; they just need a push in the right direction. They need someone there to ask them, 'What do you think the next step is and why?' or 'What do you know and what don't you know?'"

As previously stated and worth repeating, parents need to understand that their support of their child does not hinge on how much mathematics they know, but rather, the questions they pose. Good questions, such as those listed in chapter 2, can guide a child to better think through the mathematics they are learning in school.

Even if parents can't answer their child's questions at home, there is great value in parents guiding their child to form the questions that they can then ask their teacher at school. As a parent pointed out, "If my daughter and I cannot figure something out, we craft the questions she will ask her teacher the next day. When she comes home, I ask her what she found out and we learn together."

Receptiveness

Also previously noted, and worth repeating, is that parents *do* care, and *are* receptive to teachers' support. This receptiveness was particularly noted in chapter 3 while describing teachers' observations of parents posing guiding questions to their children and engaging in conversations with their children over mathematical tasks involving multiple solutions and methods of solution.

Interviews deepened teachers' awareness of both parents' and children's receptiveness to those opportunities to interact. For example, parents acknowledged the value of (a) using manipulatives to concretely represent mathematical concepts, and (b) engaging in "two-way" conversations with their child about each other's mathematical thinking. Representative comments included:

- "We share answers and talk more."
- "I learned to collaborate instead of impose my ideas on my daughter."
- "I learned not to dominate homework time."
- "I'm starting to catch myself. I listen more now before jumping in. It's not easy though; I'm used to telling. I'm getting there."

Teachers noted while observing that children were very willing to explain their thinking to their parents; the rationale for such noted enjoyment surfaced while interviewing. For example, a fourth-grader noted, "This was great; now she listens to what I think," and a fifth-grader stated, "It was hard to say what I was thinking. It kind of hurt my head. But it did help me sort things out."

Teachers became aware that parents want to communicate with teachers about their children's progress. However, as previously noted, parents' time is often limited due to job-related reasons.

While interviewing, a parent informed a teacher that she knew about her child's progress in mathematics only through the school's online student assessment reports; she didn't have time before or after school to pose the questions she had about her child's report. Other teachers found similar situations existed and decided to e-mail and/or call those parents facing time constraints.

Teachers called parents at their workplace during convenient times set up ahead of time. The phone conversations, although brief, were long enough to share with a parent how their child was progressing and ways they could improve. Teachers found parents appreciative of this form of communication, noting that they were able to ask teachers specific questions and felt more "in the loop."

Behaviors

Teachers became aware of reasons for classroom behaviors they hadn't known about prior to interviewing parents. For example, several seventh-grade parents told a teacher that their children weren't participating in class because they didn't want to "stand out as a math nerd" to their peers. Concern for one's image among peers is quite important among middle school students. They want to be perceived as "cool," and, historically, interest in and success with mathematics hasn't been a contributing factor to such an image.

Teachers also learned from some parents that their children weren't motivated to learn mathematics because they didn't see its relevance in real life, a representative comment being "I've been hit with the question as to why math is necessary in life and all I can come up with is banking and engineering. If you could give some examples of where math is used in everyday life, I might have a better chance in getting my kids to see the purpose for mathematics."

Receiving this "inside information," as one teacher referred to it, influenced the teachers to infuse more applications of mathematics into classroom conversations. Careers that use mathematics, and popular figures in society who use mathematics in their careers, were brought into their mathematics lessons as well. At school meetings, parents were called upon to assist in promoting a better image for mathematics.

Another enlightening moment came when some teachers found that their classroom parents were having their children explain to them at home the problems and methods taught in school. This was a way for parents to learn the content themselves. A parent who makes it a practice to pose *why* and *how* questions to her daughter stated, "Since I do not know many math terms, I ask my daughter to express her work in different ways. I am actually learning a lot from her." This feedback sparked teachers to think about ways to have children support parents at home as a means for building parents' content knowledge and reducing feelings of isolation.

Teachers started assigning students mathematics content to teach to their parents. Children were charged with (a) explaining content learned in school to their parents at home; (b) giving their parents a related example to complete; (c) checking parents' answers and listening to their approaches; and (d) providing their parents with feedback.

This was a productive practice that parents had started, and upon knowing about it, teachers were able to intervene and enhance that practice. Children were able to review material learned in school, support their parents' content knowledge, and have follow-up classroom conversations about mathematical thinking that included and respected parents' contributions.

Another teacher intervened upon learning from a seventh-grade mother that she checks the school's website every day for homework assignments. The mother would make a chart with her daughter's homework assignments written out for her daughter to see when she arrived home from school. The teacher advised the parent to adjust this practice. Rather than recording the assignments for her daughter, the teacher suggested that the child copy all of the assignments onto the chart herself and cross them off on her own, once completed. This framework allowed the parent to monitor her daughter's activity in a way that also held her daughter accountable for her work.

Several teachers learned from parents they interviewed that their children resist their efforts to try to share a different way of approaching a mathematics problem. "This is not how my teacher told me to solve this!" and "We did it differently in class!" were common household statements parents heard. In response, teachers conveyed to their students that discussing different approaches with their parents helps deepen everyone's understanding of a mathematics problem.

To cultivate this type of communication, one teacher started assigning her students a homework example to do with their parent(s). Students were responsible for (a) sharing their approach with their parent(s) and (b) investigating their parent(s) approach. During a follow-up lesson in school, the teacher facilitated a discussion among students that involved them comparing and contrasting the approaches with one another, as well as looking for connections among them.

Such an approach is one recommended by Marta Civil, a leader of parental engagement in mathematics education (Civil and Menendez-Radford, 2010). This teacher found the strategy helpful in developing her students' appreciation for diverse ways of thinking about mathematics.

Unfortunately, some teachers discovered a group of parents viewing academic achievement as solely the responsibility of the school. These parents didn't acknowledge their role in the learning process at all. The teacher's strategy previously described can respond to such a challenging circumstance. By bringing differing approaches from home into the mathematics classroom, as she did, children's learning is enriched by other parents, if not their own.

Cultivating parental engagement can be a complex process. Several variables are at play, and there aren't always easy answers. However, by knowing the circumstances that exist, you as teacher can begin to take steps toward confronting the complexities you learn about through inquiry.

Planning Your Interview Inquiry

- Interviewing, when conducted in conjunction with surveying and observing, provides opportunities for the teacher inquirer to (a) clarify and/or expand upon survey response(s) and (b) investigate reasons for the parent-child interactions observed. Interviewing can also serve as a means for investigating parents' reactions and suggestions concerning the support you provide for them.

  Following are questions to ponder as you reflect on your survey and observation data.
  - What data do you want to dig deeper into?
  - What new questions do you have as a result of analyzing your survey and/or observation data?
  - For which forms of support are you interested in gathering parents' feedback?
- Interviews can be conducted with individual parents or families, or with groups of parents or families. The choices you make depend on what you are wondering about.
  - Who will you interview, and how will you conduct your interview(s)?
  - How do you plan to process what you hear so you can respond to your findings?
- While interviewing, parents' lack of mathematics content knowledge surfaced over and over again for teachers, as well as parents' strangeness to the manner in which mathematics is taught. This finding surfaced through surveying and observing as well.
  - How would you respond if you note parents' unfamiliarity with mathematics content and pedagogy?
  - Has your response changed since you reflected on this question in chapter 2? If so, how and why?
- The teachers described in this chapter became aware that parents *do* care. Parents were receptive to their support and wanted to communicate about their child's progress. However, parents' time was found to be limited due to job-related reasons.
  - How would you respond if you note parents' time constraints?
- Teachers became aware of reasons for children's behaviors they hadn't known about prior to interviewing parents. Teachers learned about parents' actions that warranted their intervention.
  - What student behaviors do you wonder about?

- ♦ What parent actions might you investigate?
- Once you have collected your interview data, your analysis of that data begins, and the story you are telling becomes even more detailed. As previously recommended, take your field notes and simply read through them once or twice. Use the same questions from previous chapters to start making sense of the responses you gather through interviewing.
  - ♦ Why did I collect this data about parents in the first place?
  - ♦ What do I notice about the data I collected about parents?
  - ♦ How would I describe the data I collected about parents to others?
- Engage again in coding and memoing your data as explained in previous chapters.
  - ♦ What is most interesting about the data I have about parents?
  - ♦ What are some things in my data about parents that stand out from the rest?
  - ♦ How might I fit different pieces of my data about parents together?
- Reflect on still more questions from previous chapters, with a lens now focused on your interview data.
  - ♦ What have I learned about my classroom parents through interviewing?
  - ♦ What implications do my findings have on my practices concerning parents?
  - ♦ What changes might I make in how I support parents?
  - ♦ What new wonderings do I have about parents and mathematics as a result of interviewing?

Supporting Parents through the Grades

A big takeaway for teachers as a result of interviewing was their realization of the need to communicate with parents about (a) children's progress; (b) strategies for supporting children's mathematical thinking; and (c) applications of mathematics in everyday life. To help cultivate that communication, the National Council of Teachers of Mathematics provides an online *Teacher's Corner* that includes supportive teacher resources for crafting presentations to parents along with related materials to distribute to parents. You can access these resources at http://www.figurethis.org/teacher_corner .htm.

A Family Corner located at http://www.figurethis.org/family_corner.htm offers resources under categories titled Families and School, Families and Mathematics, Families and Homework, Families and Support, as well as Mathematics and Literature. In addition, mathematics challenges relevant to middle school topics titled Figure This are available at http://www.figure this.org/challenges/challenge_index.htm. These challenges engage families in real-world applications of mathematics, and include solutions and background information that help guide the entire families' understanding of the mathematics involved in each challenge.

References

Civil, M., and J. Menendez-Radford. "Involving Latino and Latina Parents in Their Children's Mathematics Education." Research Brief, posted December 20, 2010. National Council of Teachers of Mathematics.

Cresswell, J. W. *Qualitative Inquiry and Research Design*. Thousand Oaks, CA: Sage, 1998.

Patton, M. Q. *Qualitative Research & Evaluation Method*. 3rd ed. Thousand Oaks, CA: Sage, 2002.

CHAPTER FIVE

~

Anchor Tasks for Families

This chapter includes anchor tasks for connecting parents with school mathematics throughout the grades. The tasks support parents' familiarity with mathematics content and provide entry points for parents to engage in conversation with their child about mathematical thinking.

A common thread permeating the chapters of this book thus far is parents' unfamiliarity with mathematics content and methods of teaching that content. To address this recurring finding, tasks for developing parents' knowledge of mathematics content and pedagogy comprise this chapter.

These tasks are termed "anchor tasks" because they serve to connect parents to their child's learning of mathematics throughout the grades. These tasks also provide contexts for teacher inquirers to observe parent-child interactions while working together, as well as interview families to investigate their reactions to the experience.

Anchor Task 1: Concept Cards

Using concept cards, such as the one below, allows parents and children to visualize, explore, and communicate ideas. Concept cards are teaching tools that foster conceptual understandings.

These are pairs of perpendicular lines.

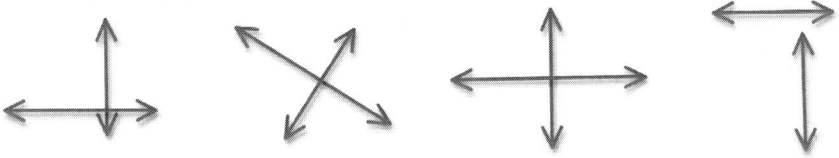

These are <u>not</u> pairs of perpendicular lines.

Which of these are perpendicular lines?

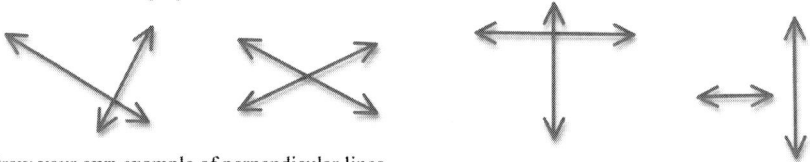

Draw your own example of perpendicular lines.

Draw your own non-example of perpendicular lines.

What are perpendicular lines?

Figure 5.1.

Examples and non-examples of a concept are illustrated with various representations. Families eliminate irrelevant characteristics and identify essential ones in order to formulate definitions that contain necessary and sufficient information.

The third part of the card requires families to distinguish between correct and incorrect examples, a task that strengthens analytical skills. Families then provide their own examples and non-examples along with their own definition. The cards at this point invite creative thinking and discourse about different possibilities and related justifications. In addition, by having families illustrate and form definitions, content material is conveyed in a manner that actively involves families in using analysis and classification skills, necessary components of algebraic thinking.

These concept cards can be designed for different topics and grade levels. Additional concept cards can be found at http://tinyurl.com/ltpw6af. Families can also be given a blank template such as the one shown below and be asked to design their own concept card to share with each other.

These are _____.

These are <u>not</u> _____.

Which of these are _____?

Draw your own example of _____.

Draw your own non-example of _____.

Figure 5.2.

Anchor Task 2: Attribute Pieces

An attribute piece set is comprised of thirty-two pieces consisting of four shapes (triangle, circle, square, and hexagon) in four colors (yellow, red, green, and blue) and two sizes (small and big). Printable attribute pieces can be found at http://tinyurl.com/ltpw6af.

Using attribute pieces with this task involves families in problem solving about how to arrange all of the pieces into a line where every piece differs from the one after it in one, two, or three ways. For example, in a one-difference line, a big red square could follow a big green square, with the one difference being color. For a two-difference line, a small yellow circle could follow a big green circle, with the two differences being size and color. For a three-difference line, a big red hexagon could follow a small blue circle, with the three differences being size, color, and shape.

Families can also investigate whether or not their attribute-piece lines can have all of the small pieces at the beginning, and reason about why or why not. The amount of pieces used and the tasks presented to families will depend on the grade level involved. As with the concept cards, this is a task that can be adapted for use throughout the grades.

Puzzles such as those below also provide opportunities for families to problem solve together using the attribute pieces.

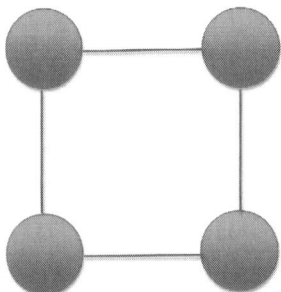

Figure 5.3.

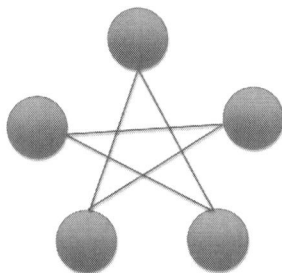

Figure 5.4.

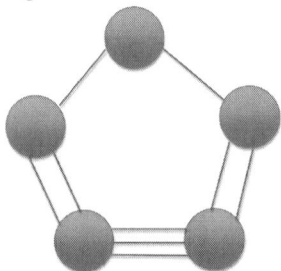

Figure 5.5.

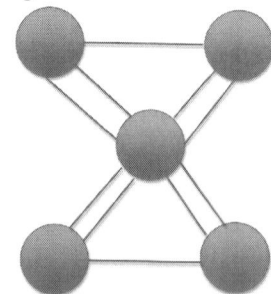

Figure 5.6.

These puzzles can be displayed on large pieces of paper or file folders. Families place an attribute piece into each of the circle areas. If the circles are connected with one line, the attribute pieces placed into those circles must differ in one way (either by size, color, or shape). If the circles are connected with two lines, the attributes pieces differ in two ways. And if the circles are connected with three lines, the attribute pieces differ in three ways. The complexity of the puzzle depends on the grade level involved.

Additional examples of attribute-piece puzzles can be found at http://tinyurl.com/ltpw6af. As with the concept cards, families can also be asked to create their own attribute piece puzzle to share with each other.

Anchor Task 3: Pattern Blocks

This task involves certain pattern blocks (yellow hexagons, red trapezoids, blue rhombi, and green triangles) and engages families in problem solving about a computational situation rooted in understanding the existing fractional relationships among the pieces. Printable pattern blocks can be found at http://mason.gmu.edu/%mmankus/Handson/manipulatives.htm.

The task is presented in the following manner.

- Distribute pattern blocks to families and initiate free play with guiding questions:
  - ◆ What pattern blocks can be joined together to form a yellow hexagon?
  - ◆ How many red trapezoids cover a yellow hexagon?
  - ◆ How many blue rhombi cover a yellow hexagon?
  - ◆ How many green triangles cover a yellow hexagon?
- Ask everyone to make a design or structure with their pattern blocks; the amount of blocks they use does not matter.
- Pose the question: How much does your design or structure cost if a green triangle costs $1.89?
- Allow exploration, questioning, and multiple strategies, and observe and guide—refrain from telling, and give hints if needed. Encourage collaboration!
- Pose the question: How much would your design cost if the green triangle now costs $2.53? (Same recommendations as in the previous step.)
- Pose the question: What change could you make to the cost of the green triangle so that the total cost of your design would now increase by more than a dollar but not more than two dollars? (Same recommendations as in the previous step.)

For families with younger children, the task can be adapted so that the green triangle costs one, two, or five cents. These families could then discuss how to make the cost of their design increase and/or decrease. Families with older children can compute with larger numbers and discuss how to make the total cost increase by more than 10% but not more than 15%.

Anchor Task 4: Perimeter and Area

This task positions families to discover a relationship between area and perimeter. With pencils and graph paper, ask families to record as many solutions as they can think of for the following task.

- You have twenty feet of fencing to create a rectangular enclosed pen for animals on a farm. How many different ways can you make an enclosed pen? What is the area of each of these different enclosed pens?

The solutions shown below portray how shapes with the same perimeter can have varying areas.

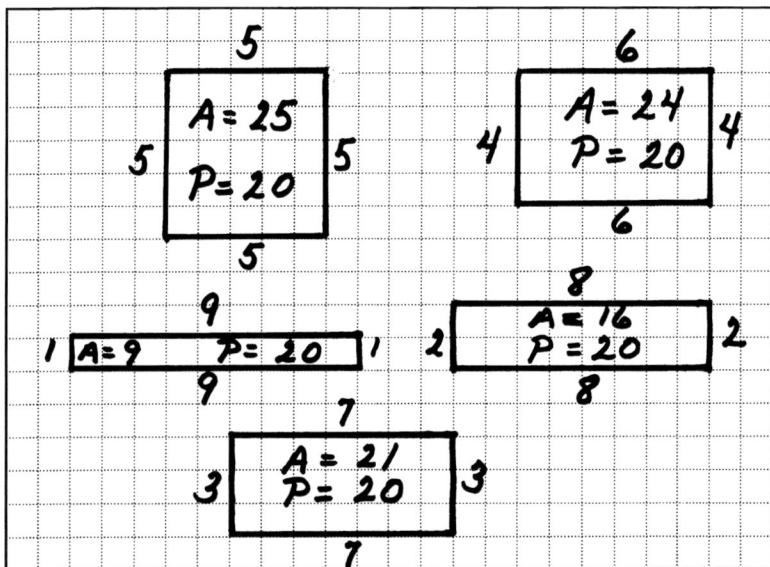

Figure 5.7.

The realization of the square shape having the largest area lends itself to discussion about real-life applications of area and perimeter. For example, one boy stated during a family engagement session where this task was used, "If I get my own room someday, I'm asking for the most square-ish one I can get. That nine-by-one design is out of the question. As soon as I get up out of bed, I'll walk into the wall."

This activity also develops understandings involving the formulas we use when finding perimeter and area of rectangles. It can be adapted so families can design animal pens with straight sides in as many ways as they can think of without having the restriction of forming rectangles. Families can count the twenty units around their shapes and develop an understanding for perimeter; they can count the corresponding squares within their shapes and develop an understanding for area.

A follow-up task to the original one could involve designing rectangular pens where the area remains constant at twenty, and families explore what happens to the corresponding perimeters. In this case, families can discover that the largest perimeter exists for the rectangle with the largest length.

Anchor Task 5: Finding Pi

This task provides an opportunity for families to discover the linear relationship that exists between the lengths of the diameter and circumference of a circle. The task is presented to families by first giving them circles of various sizes, pieces of yarn, and rulers. Families are then asked to measure the circumference and diameter of each circle to the nearest given unit.

Families record their measurements on a chart posted at the front of the room. In this chart, one column contains data for diameter measurements, another column contains data for circumference measurements, and another for answers obtained when dividing circumference measurements by their respective diameter measurements.

Once families have recorded their data on the chart, analysis of that data begins. Pose the following questions to guide the conversation.

- What do you notice about the quotients obtained from division?
- What does this tell us about the relationship between a circle's circumference and diameter?
- How can we write an equation to explain that relationship between a circle's circumference and diameter?

Such a conversation builds conceptual understandings about pi being the constant of proportionality between the diameter and circumference of circles since the quotients will all tend toward 3.14. To transition from representing pi in an algebraic equation to representing pi on a coordinate axes, ask families to plot the chart data on a coordinate axes with diameter representing x values and circumference representing y values.

Pose the following questions:

- How do the points (x, y) help us explain the relationship (behavior) between a circle's circumference and diameter?
- What other linear relationships do you think exist in our world?

These questions cultivate conversation about pi serving as the slope of the line of best fit that can be drawn once the points are plotted, representing the linear behavior of the diameter and circumference of a circle. Other real-life examples of linear relationships are a person's foot length and height, Celsius versus Fahrenheit temperatures, interest rates, and foreign currencies.

This task, in its entirety, is relevant for middle school families. Adaptations can be made, though, for families of lower-grade levels. For example, families can engage in measuring circumference and diameter of different size circles, and look for patterns among the data they gather. Such an investigation helps guide families to concretely gain understandings about diameter and circumference, as well as discover how the diameter measurements are smaller than the corresponding circumference measurements.

Families are also positioned to note how both the diameter and circumference measurements increase as the circle size increases. Where appropriate, families can divide the circumference measurements by corresponding diameter measurements to note how the quotients all tend toward 3.14.

Anchor Task 6: Monster Combos

This task engages parents and children in exploring combinations. By joining the different heads, bodies, and feet shown below to create a monster, families concretely develop understanding for the meaning of a combination.

These monster parts can be found at http://tinyurl.com/ltpw6af and cut out for families to manipulate the pieces. An example of one of twelve possible monsters is shown below.

Head #1

Head #2

Monster # 1

Body #1

Body #2

Body #3

Head #1

Body #1

Feet #1

Feet #1

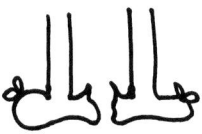

Feet #2

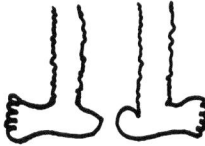

Figure 5.8.   **Figure 5.9.**

Families can create and pictorially represent all twelve monsters. You can then ask families to investigate how to determine the total number of possible combinations numerically.

Guide families to see how they can arrive at the answer of twelve by multiplying the number of possible heads (two) by the number of possible bodies (three) by the number of possible feet (two). Families will have discovered the Counting Principle for determining the number of possible combinations.

While this task as written is appropriate for grades three and four, younger grades can also engage in this activity by concretely building the different monsters and using fewer pieces as appropriate. In addition, a related interactive tool for grades pre–K through five, titled Bobbie Bear, can be found on the National Council of Teachers of Mathematics website at http://illuminations.nctm.org/Activity.aspx?id=3540.

Monster combos can also be adapted for older grades. Consider contexts such as creating sandwiches, coffee drinks, outfits, or license plates. Provide the related choices for each context and incorporate other representations of the possible combinations using lists and tree diagrams. Whatever grade level you are working with, or context you are using, the objective is for families to concretely discover the systematic procedure for finding and representing the total number of possible combinations. Such a setting allows parents to engage in a learning environment that reflects their child's mathematics classroom; one where students construct understandings for mathematical ideas and procedures rather than memorize what is merely told to them.

Anchor Task 7: Let's Talk Pizza!

Building upon this objective of concretely making sense of the mathematical ideas and procedures we use, this task offers a real-life context for building understandings about fractions and the procedure we use when multiplying them. The context to share with families is as follows:

> I plan on making my own Sicilian pizza. I'm going to cut it into small pieces to serve at a party. I'll make a quarter of it without cheese because some of my friends don't like cheese. One of my friends loves mushrooms, but does not like cheese. So I'll make sure that a fifth of the part without cheese has mushrooms on it. What part of my whole Sicilian pizza will have mushrooms and no cheese on it?

After reviewing the context with families and making clarifications where needed, ask families to represent the pizza and its components in order to arrive at a solution. After allowing time for families to work on this task together, facilitate a whole-group conversation about the task. Elicit from families the need to first represent the pizza in fourths, and then the fourth with no cheese on it as follows:

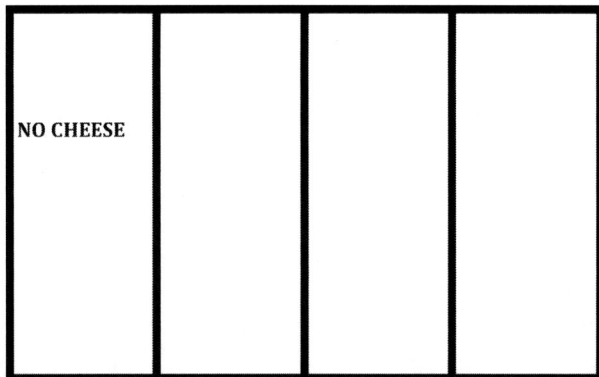

Figure 5.10.

Transition the conversation to representing fifths on the pizza, and then the fifth that has mushrooms on it but no cheese as follows:

NO CHEESE			
NO CHEESE			
NO CHEESE			
NO CHEESE			
NO CHEESE			

Figure 5.11.

After visualizing the answer of 1/20, ask families to discuss how to arrive at this answer numerically so as to determine the procedure we follow for multiplying fractions. Seeing the following numerical calculation along with its representation justifies the procedure of multiplying the numerators and multiplying the denominators to arrive at the answer.

NO CHEESE			
NO CHEESE			
NO CHEESE ✖			
NO CHEESE			
NO CHEESE			

Figure 5.12. $\frac{1}{5}$ **of** $\frac{1}{4} = \frac{1}{20}$

A PowerPoint presentation for your use with parents can be found at http://tinyurl.com/ltpw6af.

CHAPTER SIX

~

Learning as a Teacher Inquiry Group about Parents and Mathematics

In this chapter, teachers' collective inquiry concerning parents and mathematics is explained. Two professional learning frameworks for you and your colleagues to use are described. One framework focuses on using survey, observation, and/or interview findings about parents and mathematics; the other, on using best-practice publications about parents and mathematics. Guidelines for structuring a Teacher Inquiry Group are provided, and related questions for guiding that group's collective learning are offered.

> *Participating in a teacher inquiry group developed our habits of mind for supporting parents with mathematics.*
>
> *Kindergarten Teacher, Staten Island, New York*

Teacher education programs prepare you, as teacher, with up-to-date knowledge, skills, and dispositions necessary for effective teaching. However, your professional learning hinges on support structures for such learning within schools.

Research shows that establishing long-term conditions that allow teachers to learn continuously from one another within schools is among the most effective ways to support teacher learning (Heck, Banilower, Weiss, and Rosenberg 2008). In fact, such learning opportunities are the most important factors for improving teacher practice (Borko 2004).

This chapter includes descriptions of two frameworks for supporting you and your colleagues' professional learning with a lens focused on parents and mathematics. Previous chapters in this book were written to guide your individual inquiry about parents and mathematics. This chapter supports collective inquiry as what I term a Teacher Inquiry Group.

A Teacher Inquiry Group is meant to refer to a group of teachers that meets regularly, shares findings, and works collaboratively toward an objective; for this book's purpose, that objective is to know and support parents with mathematics. The first professional learning framework involves group members' inquiry findings from surveys, observations, and/or interviewing. It is hybrid in nature, meaning group meetings are both in person and virtual.

The second professional learning framework shares the same objective as the first, with this framework involving group members using best-practice publications about parents and mathematics. These publications are stepping stones from which group members' inquiry efforts stem.

Both frameworks (a) provide long-term support of teacher learning; (b) develop leadership skills; and (c) cultivate teacher inquiry as a means for knowing and supporting parents with mathematics.

Collective Learning Framework 1

In this framework, a Teacher Inquiry Group shares data they gather through surveying, observing, and/or interviewing. The first step, as with the other framework described later in this chapter, is to form a Teacher Inquiry Group. Once a group of your colleagues who are interested in learning more about parents and mathematics is formed, take the following steps to craft your inquiry journey.

Determine the most appropriate time to meet in person. Strive to meet for ninety-minute intervals, and schedule meetings with enough time in between so that group members can (a) collectively plan their inquiry journey in person; (b) individually gather data; (c) virtually report/discuss findings in the form of blog postings; and (d) collectively discuss responsive action steps in person.

Assign group members to serve as facilitators for the in-person conversations on a rotating basis. This allows group members to gain experience in leading colleagues' professional growth; teacher leadership is an essential ingredient in any kind of lasting reform (Franke, Kazemi, and Battey 2007).

Set a direction for the group by determining an aspect(s) of parents and mathematics the group as a whole will seek to investigate.

Once you have your group members selected, and two in-person meeting times and facilitators determined, you and your colleagues are ready to embark on your inquiry journey!

First Meeting

At this first in-person meeting, the selected facilitator guides the group in forming a question about parents and mathematics that is specific and manageable enough to answer. Some sample questions from teachers I have worked with follow.

- How do parents engage in their child's mathematical learning?
- What challenges do parents face concerning their child's mathematical learning?
- How can a school mathematics initiative focused on manipulatives cultivate parent-child collaboration?
- What areas of mathematics are parents most concerned about and why?
- What forms of support do parents want concerning their child's learning of mathematics?
- Do parents talk with their child about real-life applications of mathematics? If so, how?
- What types of questions do parents pose to their children when assisting them with mathematics?

The next decision the group makes at this first meeting is their inquiry approach (surveying, observing, and/or interviewing). As previously explained, using all three inquiry approaches can yield rich findings and responsive action steps tailored to families' specific skill sets and needs.

Individual group members are then charged with collecting and analyzing their findings, and virtually submitting blog postings by due dates agreed upon by the group members at the first meeting. This transition to virtual conversation allows each group member to (a) post their findings for group members to read; (b) thoroughly read group members' postings; and (c) respond to group members' postings prior to the second in-person meeting.

Several free blogging platforms exist for online communication purposes. One I suggest is Blogger (www.blogger.com). Following are suggested guidelines for blog postings that group members can use when documenting and responding to each other's findings. The guidelines include suggested questions related to surveying, observing, and interviewing that require detailed responses. A word limit is suggested to help focus bloggers' comments.

Blog Post Guidelines for Reporting Survey Findings

First Post
Using the responses from your parent surveys, answer the following questions in no more than 250 words.

- How and for what reasons do your parents primarily assist their children with mathematics?
- How and for what reasons do your parents want teachers to assist them with mathematics?

Additional Posts
After reading others' first posts, provide feedback to at least two of your colleagues in no more than 150 words.

Blog Post Guidelines for Reporting Observation Findings

First Post
Using your field notes, answer the following questions in no more than 250 words.

- How were parents explaining to their child and/or exploring ideas?
- What short answer, prompting, and/or probing questions were parents asking their child?
- How were parents positive and/or negative in their tone of communication with their child?
- What reason(s) do you think account for what you observed?

Additional Posts
After reading others' first posts, provide feedback to at least two of your colleagues in no more than 150 words.

Blog Post Guidelines for Reporting Interview Findings

First Post
Using your field notes, answer the following questions in no more than 250 words.

- How and for what reasons do parents primarily assist their child with mathematics?

- What challenges do parents face when assisting their child with mathematics?
- How and for what reasons do parents want teachers to assist them with mathematics?

Additional Posts
After reading others' first posts, provide feedback to at least two of your colleagues in no more than 150 words.

Second Meeting

At the second in-person meeting, group members come ready to brainstorm about action steps that respond to the group's findings. The facilitator initiates conversation among group members by posing the following questions.

- In what ways was the information we gathered new knowledge for you?
- In what ways does the information we gathered impact upon how we support parents with mathematics?

From this discussion should stem responsive action steps that the group can implement and assess. And, since inquiry is a cyclical process, group members may very well find themselves with new wonderings to investigate. An example of such a newfound wondering occurred for a group of teachers when they found a sizeable number of parents hiring tutors for their children. The teachers wondered why. Was it the quality of classroom instruction? Were parents too busy? Did parents just not know how to help?

After digging deeper, the teachers unfortunately discovered that these parents viewed education as teachers' (classroom teacher or tutor) sole responsibility. A representative comment was: "I send my child to school to learn. That's the school's job, not mine." These teachers continue to grapple with ways to respond to such a mindset. There are no easy answers; however, uncovering such an issue is an example of how teacher inquiry can direct teachers and school administrators to areas that warrant attention.

Collective Learning Framework 2

The second professional learning framework shared with you in this chapter involves teachers collectively using best-practice publications about parents and mathematics. Gather a group of colleagues who are interested in finding out what educators outside of their own school have learned about parents and mathematics.

As a Teacher Inquiry Group, organize your conversations by taking the following steps.

- Determine the most appropriate time to meet in person. Strive to meet twice a month for ninety minutes so as to have enough time for rich conversations.
- Take turns serving as facilitator for the same leadership reasons explained when describing Framework 1.
- Select an article to focus your conversations around.

Listed below are titles of articles about parents and mathematics from journals published by the National Council of Teachers of Mathematics (NCTM); complete citations can be found in this chapter's reference section. The content of the articles is applicable across grade levels. Please note, though, that a vast amount of grade-specific articles on parental engagement are also available in the journals published by the National Council of Teachers of Mathematics.

These journals can be found at www.nctm.org under the tab for Journals & Books. *Teaching Children Mathematics* focuses on grades pre–K through grade five. *Mathematics Teaching in the Middle School* focuses on grades six through eight, while *Mathematics Teacher* focuses on grades nine through twelve. In addition, conducting a search for parents and mathematics within the NCTM website will yield all available resources this organization offers teachers for supporting parents with mathematics.

Suggested Article Titles

- "Addressing Parents' Concerns about Mathematics Reform"
- "An Educator's Guide to Answering Parents' Questions on Mathematics"
- "Beyond Helping with Homework: Parents and Children Doing Mathematics at Home"
- "Identifying Opportunities to Connect Parents, Students, and Mathematics"
- "Technology from the Classroom: Creating Digital Partnerships with Parents"
- "Family Math Nights: Collaborative Celebrations of Mathematical Learning"

- "A Teacher's Journal: The M.O.O.K. Book: Students Author a Book about Mathematics"
- "Families Ask: Homework: How Much Help Is Enough?"
- "Quick Reads: Promising Partnerships: Learning 24–7: Changing Attitudes about Mathematics"
- "Families Ask: Showing Your Work: Beyond Following Steps"
- "Parental Involvement in the Reform of Mathematics Education"
- "Sound Off! Parents Are Not the Enemy: Ten Tips for Improving Parent-Teacher Communication"
- "Involving Latino and Latina Parents in Their Children's Mathematics Education"

Upon forming your Teacher Inquiry Group and determining meeting times, a facilitator, and an article, distribute the article to group members. Each member then reads the article and prepares for a conversation one week later about the article's main points.

First Meeting

At the first meeting, the facilitator is charged with engaging the group in dialogue about the main points of the article, and how the article's content might be applied to the group members' classroom parents/families. The facilitator should restate group members' expressed view and ask for clarification as needed. The facilitator can also offer a different perspective for group members to consider. In addition, to cultivate the most comprehensive conversation, the facilitator should pose questions about aspects of the article that haven't emerged during the conversation. Such guided dialogue cultivates self-directedness, a necessary characteristic for professional growth (Sutton, Burroughs, and Yopp 2011).

Classroom Application

The next step is to shift the conversation to group members' classrooms. Group members are charged with (a) applying an aspect of the discussed article with their classroom parents/families, and (b) investigating its impact using one or more of the inquiry approaches discussed in this book.

Second Meeting

Approximately two weeks later, the same facilitator guides another conversation, during which each group member (a) shares how he/she used the article, and (b) reports on their inquiry findings. The group may decide to apply the article's content as a school initiative rather than to individual classrooms. In this case, the conversation should include each group member's contribution to that initiative and their related findings.

Teachers who used this framework expressed to me that their conversations increased awareness of parental engagement inside and outside of their own classrooms. The teachers valued the opportunities the framework offered them to learn about teacher and parent approaches at various grade levels. In addition, the teachers stated that the conversations served as a forum for sharing challenges and ways of confronting them. As indicated in this chapter's opening quote, teachers commented that reading publications, implementing the strategies in them, and sharing resulting experiences with colleagues helped them develop good professional habits of mind for supporting parents with mathematics.

References

Bay-Williams, J. "Families Ask: Showing Your Work: Beyond Following Steps." *Mathematics Teaching in the Middle School* 12, no. 6 (2007): 338–39.

Borko, H. "Professional Development and Teacher Learning: Mapping the Terrain." *Educational Researcher* 33, no. 8 (2004): 3–15.

Chapman, S. "A Teacher's Journal: The M.O.O.K. Book: Students Author a Book about Mathematics." *Teaching Children Mathematics* 6, no. 6 (2000): 388–90.

Coates, G. D., and K. Mayfield, eds. "Families Ask: Homework: How Much Help Is Enough?" *Mathematics Teaching in the Middle School* 15, no. 5 (2009): 292–93.

Fagan, N. "Identifying Opportunities to Connect Parents, Students, and Mathematics." *Teaching Children Mathematics* 15, no. 1 (2008): 6–9.

Franke, M., E. Kazemi, and D. Battey. "Mathematics Teaching and Classroom Practice." In *Second Handbook of Research on Mathematics Teaching and Learning Mathematics Teaching in the Middle School*, edited by F. K. Lester Jr. Charlotte, NC: Information Age Publishing 2007, 225–56.

Hawes, K. "Sound Off! Parents Are Not the Enemy: Ten Tips for Improving Parent-Teacher Communication." *Mathematics Teacher* 101, no. 5 (2007): 329–31.

Heck, D. J., I. R. Banilower, E. R. Weiss, and S. Rosenberg. "Studying the Effects of Professional Development: The Case of the NSF's Local Systemic Change through Teacher Enhancement Initiative." *Journal for Research in Mathematics Education* 39, no. 2 (2008): 113–52.

Hendrickson, S., D. Siebert, S. Smith, H. Kunzler, and S. Christensen. "Addressing Parents' Concerns about Mathematics Reform." *Teaching Children Mathematics* 11, no. 1 (2004): 18–23.

Kliman, M. "Beyond Helping with Homework: Parents and Children Doing Mathematics at Home." *Teaching Children Mathematics* 6, no. 3 (1999): 140–46.

Pagni, D. "An Educator's Guide to Answering Parents' Questions on Mathematics." *Teaching Children Mathematics* 7, no. 1 (2000): 44–46.

Peressini, D. "Parental Involvement in the Reform of Mathematics Education," *Mathematics Teacher* 90, no. 6 (1997): 421–25.

Ross, M. "Technology from the Classroom: Creating Digital Partnerships with Parents." *Teaching Children Mathematics* 18, no. 4 (2011): 260–62.

Shannon-Smith, E., and G. Fawcett. "Quick Reads: Promising Partnerships: Learning 24-7: Changing Attitudes about Mathematics." *Mathematics Teaching in the Middle School* 14, no. 2 (2008): 108–9.

Sutton, J., E. Burroughs, and D. Yopp. "Mathematics Coaching Knowledge: Domains and Definitions." *Journal of Mathematics Education Leadership* 13, no. 2 (2011): 13–20.